ESSENTIAL
NEW YORK

★ Best places to see 34–55

■ Featured sight

00563191

Midtown Manhattan 85–104

Empire State Building to
Greenwich Village 127–146

Uptown and Central Park 105–126

Lower Manhattan 147–165

Written by Mick Sinclair
Updated by Donna Dailey

© Automobile Association Developments Limited 2009
First published 2007
Reprinted 2009. Information verified and updated

ISBN: 978-0-7495-6016-4

Published by AA Publishing, a trading name of Automobile Association Developments
Limited, whose registered office is Fanum House, Basing View, Basingstoke,
Hampshire RG21 4EA. Registered number 1878835.

Colour separation: MRM Graphics Ltd
Printed and bound in Italy by Printer Trento S.r.l.

A03616
Maps in this title produced from cartographic data © Tele Atlas N.V. 2005 Tele Atlas
Transport map © Communicarta Ltd, UK

About this book

This book is divided into six sections.

The essence of New York pages 6–19
Introduction; Features; Food and drink; Short break including the 10 Essentials

Planning pages 20–33
Before you go; Getting there; Getting around; Being there

Best places to see pages 34–55
The unmissable highlights of any visit to New York

Best things to do pages 56–81
Great cafés; stunning views; places to take the children and more

Exploring pages 82–165
The best places to visit in New York, organized by area

Excursions pages 166–183
Places to visit out of town

Maps
All map references are to the maps on the covers. For example, SoHo has the reference 🞡 J19 – indicating the grid square in which it is to be found.

Admission prices
Inexpensive (under $5)
Moderate ($5–$10)
Expensive (over $10)

Hotel prices
A room per night: **$** budget (under $200);
$$ moderate ($200–$400);
$$$ expensive to luxury (over $400)

Restaurant prices
A 3-course meal per person without drinks: **$** budget (under $25);
$$ moderate ($25–$50);
$$$ expensive (over $50)

♛ to ♛♛♛♛ denotes AAA rating

Contents

4

BEST THINGS TO DO

56 – 81

EXPLORING...

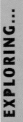

82 – 165

EXCURSIONS

166 – 183

The essence of...

Many visitors arrive in New York already knowing exactly what they want to do and see. Climbing skyscrapers, going to Broadway shows, shopping, touring world-class museums, and staying in luxury hotels can all be accomplished in New York with perhaps more style and glamour than in any other city. Yet New York is a city of infinite guises, where contrasting side-by-side neighborhoods house people from seemingly every nation on earth and where local markets, secret parks, one-room museums, and unsung architectural marvels await discovery at every turn once the obvious destinations have been exhausted.

features

Probably no city in the world is as economically powerful, as ethnically diverse, as sung about, talked about, written about, photographed, filmed, eulogized, mythologized, loved, and loathed—or simply as famous—as New York.

This city is a magnet not only for tourists but also for small-town Americans seeking the professional opportunities only New York holds, or for the chance to pursue unconventional lifestyles without fear of ridicule.

As well as transforming lives, New York regularly transforms itself. The 1980s and 1990s saw an office-building boom while more localized development saw the regeneration of SoHo, TriBeCa, Chelsea, and Times Square. Meanwhile, the Financial District recovers steadily from the devastation of September 11, 2001.

The best thing a New York visitor can do is just join in. Ride the subways and the buses, explore the nooks and crannies of offbeat neighborhoods, and discover why nobody can ever accuse New York of being boring.

You can easily swap the concrete face of the city for greener surroundings by discovering the many parks and protected wildlife habitats that lie not far from busy Manhattan. Staten Island holds some of

the city's most diverse and accessible unspoiled land. Known as the Greenbelt it spans a variety of habitats. The Gateway National Recreation Area stretches from Brooklyn and Queens, where the marshy islands and shoreline of shallow Jamaica Bay form the Jamaica Bay Wildlife Refuge, a 7-mile-long (11km) barrier peninsula on the north coast of New Jersey.

GEOGRAPHY
- Area of New York City: 321sq miles (823km sq)
- Area of Manhattan: 23sq miles (59km sq)
- Miles of street: 6,400 (10,322km)
- Miles of waterfront: 578 (932km)

PUBLIC TRANSPORTATION
- Number of subway stations: 468
- Number of subway cars: 6,200
- Buses: 6,202
- Weekday subway riders: 4.9 million

POPULATION
- The Bronx: 1.4 million
- Brooklyn: 2.5 million
- Manhattan: 1.6 million
- Queens: 2.2 million
- Staten Island: 477,000

ETHNICITY
- White: 3.6 million
- African-American: 2.1 million
- Hispanic: 2.2 million
- Asian: 963,000
- Other: 1.2 million

food & drink

Food and where to eat it is a major issue in New York, simply because competition is intense and New Yorkers have an abundance of food choices. With more than 4,000 restaurants in Manhattan alone, this is a city where you eat what you want, when you want, and do so at a price to suit all budgets.

BREAKFAST

A New York breakfast can mean dropping into a no-frills coffee shop for a substantial omelette with a seemingly endless choice of fillings, a plate of bacon and eggs or pancakes; in Chinatown it could mean a bowl of noodles or egg or even chicken porridge. In more health-conscious establishments, breakfast can be a bowl of cereal and fruit served with a choice of quality teas and freshly squeezed fruit juices.

For a New Yorker in a rush, which on a weekday is most of them most of the time, breakfast can simply be coffee "to go" and a Danish pastry, doughnut, or a bagel from the local deli. Some hotel restaurants serve breakfast, though this is rarely included in the room rate; some offer "continental" breakfast, usually consisting of coffee or tea and a muffin and/or bagel.

LUNCH

On weekdays, many restaurants offer attractively priced lunch specials, the cheapest generally around $5. A number of ethnic restaurants, chiefly Indian, present diners with an all-you-can-eat buffet. Most Chinese restaurants serve dim sum at lunchtime: bite-size buns and dumplings filled with vegetables, meat or seafood ordered from passing trolleys. Lunchcarts offering hot dogs or various ethnic fare dot the streets in areas with lots of pedestrians.

American staples such as burgers, steaks and seafood served in generous portions are the basic fare of many theme restaurants in and around Times Square. Regional U.S. cuisines such as Cajun, Creole, Southwestern, soulfood and Tex-Mex are also available for lunch and dinner.

INTERNATIONAL CUISINE

Reflecting the ethnic diversity of its population, the city also holds a whole range of international cuisines—Argentine, Brazilian, Chilean, Colombian, Chinese, Cuban, French, German, Greek, Indian, Italian, Japanese, Jewish Kosher, Korean, Mexican, Moroccan, Russian, Ukrainian, Spanish and Thai—to name but a few.

At the top end of the dining spectrum, New York's finest restaurants not only employ the world's best chefs but back them up with the top waiters and expensively designed interiors. The city has its share of food buffs ready to spend a week's wages on a meal in such surrounds, and most top-class restaurants require a reservation (sometimes weeks in advance) and appropriate attire.

DRINKS

Deciding what to drink is almost as difficult as deciding what to eat. Diners serve coffee in endless free refills, but coffee can also be available as espresso or cappuccino in a variety of flavors and blends, and in regular and decaffeinated forms. Nowadays tea is growing in popularity, and many cafés and restaurants offer hot or iced tea in a choice of flavors.

The majority of restaurants and bars serve a wide range of wines and liquors. Most serve quality beers, stocking an excellent selection from the country's growing number of microbreweries, as well as importing popular lagers from Europe. A number of places even brew their own beer on the premises.

short break

If you have only a short time to visit New York and would like to take home some unforgettable memories you can do something local and capture the real flavor of the city. The following suggestions will give you a wide range of sights and experiences that won't take very long, won't cost very much and will make your visit very special. If you only have time to choose just one of these, you will have found the true heart of the city.

● **Visit Wall Street and the site of the World Trade Center,** a haunting presence since September 11, 2001, a day that will linger in the memory of New Yorkers for generations to come (➤ 160).

- **Go to the 86th-floor observation level,** or higher still to the 102nd-floor observatory, of the Empire State Building. The city's tallest building has fabulous art deco features to rival the stupendous views (➤ 40–41).

- **Walk, bicycle, rollerblade or jog** through at least some of Central Park, one of the world's largest urban parks and without which Manhattan really would be a concrete jungle (➤ 36–37).

- **Walk across the Brooklyn Bridge** (➤ 148–149), a major engineering feat of the 19th century, which provides wonderful views of the Financial District skyline from across the East River.

- **Take the ferry** from Battery Park to Liberty Island to see the great views of New York Harbor and tour the statue, grounds and pedestal (➤ 52–53).

- **Go to a Broadway** show but don't pay full price; make use of the discount ticket booths in Times Square (➤ 54–55) and South Street Seaport (➤ 158).

- **Ride the Staten Island ferry** for outstanding views of Lower Manhattan.

- **Hang the expense** and have a drink or dinner and dancing at Rockefeller Center's Rainbow Room (➤ 92).

- **Stroll around Greenwich Village** on a Sunday afternoon and enjoy a snack in the heart of the area, Washington Square Park.

- **Gaze at** Monet's *Water Lilies* or Van Gogh's *Starry Night* at the Museum of Modern Art (➤ 50–51), even if you look at nothing else.

Planning

00563191

Before you go

WHEN TO GO

JAN	FEB	MAR	APR	MAY	JUN	JUL	AUG	SEP	OCT	NOV	DEC
4°C	5°C	8°C	16°C	21°C	27°C	29°C	28°C	25°C	19°C	12°C	4°C
39°F	41°F	46°F	61°F	70°F	80°F	84°F	82°F	77°F	66°F	54°F	39°F

● High season   ● Low season

The temperatures given in the above chart are the average daily maximum for each month. Average minimum temperatures are typically 15–20°F (8–11°C) lower. The best times of the year for pleasant weather are May, early June, September and early to mid-October. In July and August the temperatures can soar to more than 86°F (30°C), sometimes reaching 95°F (35°C) or more. Humidity can be up to 90 percent.

Every few years the city has a blizzard during the winter but generally the total annual snowfall is less than 2ft (61cm). When snow does fall in quantity, life in the city is rarely disrupted.

For information and weather reports visit www.cnn.com/weather.

WHAT YOU NEED

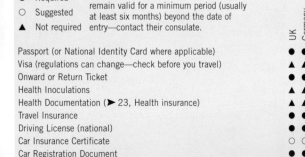

	UK	Germany	USA	Netherlands	Spain
● Required — Some countries require a passport to remain valid for a minimum period (usually at least six months) beyond the date of entry—contact their consulate.					
○ Suggested					
▲ Not required					
Passport (or National Identity Card where applicable)	●	●	▲	●	●
Visa (regulations can change—check before you travel)	▲	▲	▲	▲	▲
Onward or Return Ticket	●	●	▲	●	●
Health Inoculations	▲	▲	▲	▲	▲
Health Documentation (► 23, Health insurance)	▲	▲	▲	▲	▲
Travel Insurance	●	●	▲	●	●
Driving License (national)	●	●	●	●	●
Car Insurance Certificate	○	○	●	○	○
Car Registration Document	●	●	●	●	●

WEBSITES

NYC & Company:
www.nycvisit.com
Metropolitan TransitAuthority:
www.mta.info

The Official New York City
Website: www.nyc.gov
The Official New York State
Website: www.iloveny.com

TOURIST OFFICES AT HOME

In the U.S.A.
NYC & Company
810 Seventh Avenue
New York NY 10019
☎ 1-800/NYC-VISIT

In Australia
Trade Advisory and Consular
Assistance
☎ (300) 139 281;
www.smartraveller.gov.au

In the U.K.
NYC & Company
c/o Hills Balfour Synergy
Colechurch House
1 London Bridge Walk
London SE1 2SX
☎ (020) 7367 0900

In Canada
Consular Affairs Bureau
☎ 800/267-6788 or 613/944-6788;
www.voyage.gc.ca

HEALTH INSURANCE

Hospital emergency rooms are open 24 hours daily. There are also walk-in clinics particularly in Midtown Manhattan. Health insurance coverage of at least $1 million is strongly recommended. If involved in an accident in New York you will receive treatment by medical services and be charged later. Dental coverage is usually included.

TIME DIFFERENCES

GMT	New York	Germany	USA (LA)	Netherlands	Spain
12 noon	7AM	1PM	4AM	1PM	1PM

New York is on Eastern Standard Time, which is five hours behind Greenwich Mean Time (GMT-5). Daylight Saving Time (GMT-4) comes into operation from early March (when clocks are advanced by one hour) and runs through early November.

NATIONAL HOLIDAYS

Jan 1 *New Year's Day*
Jan (third Mon) *Martin Luther King Day*
Feb (third Mon) *Presidents Day*
Mar 17 *St. Patrick's Day*
Mar/Apr *Easter (half day Good Friday, Easter Monday whole day)*

May (last Mon) *Memorial Day*
Jul 4 *Independence Day*
Sep (first Mon) *Labor Day*
Oct (second Mon) *Columbus Day*
Nov 11 *Veterans' Day*
Late Nov *Thanksgiving (4th Thu of month)*

Dec 25 *Christmas Day*
Banks, businesses, museums and most shops are closed on these days.

Boxing Day (December 26) is not a national holiday in the U.S.

WHAT'S ON WHEN

January/February *Chinese New Year:* Parades in and around Chinatown; actual date accords with the lunar cycle.
Martin Luther King Day Parade: Along Fifth Avenue between 61st and 86th streets.

March/April *St Patrick's Day Parade:* Massive march of Irish and would-be Irish along Fifth Avenue, with countless related events.
Easter Promenade: Outrageous Easter bonnets paraded along Fifth Avenue.
Cherry Blossom Festival: Centered on Central Park's Conservatory Garden and Brooklyn's Botanic Garden.
Opening day of the baseball season: At Yankee and Shea Stadiums.

May *Bike New York Five Boro Bike Tour:* Thousands of cyclists of all levels ride through the city.
Ninth Avenue International Food Festival: A cornucopia of culinary delights on sale at stands along Ninth Avenue between 37th and 57th streets, plus musical entertainment.

June *Lesbian and Gay Pride Day:* Enormous march along Fifth Avenue from Midtown Manhattan to Washington Square; many related events throughout Greenwich Village.
National Puerto Rican Day: Parade along Fifth Avenue between 44th and 86th streets.

Shakespeare in the Park: Works of the Bard staged for free in Central Park's Delacorte Theater; continues into August.
Museum Mile Festival: Nine museums along Fifth Avenue stay open late for a mile-long block party.

July *Independence Day:* Celebrated with special activities throughout the city and fireworks over the East River.

August/September *Harlem Week:* Special events marking Harlem's history and culture.
U.S. Open Tennis Tournament: The last of the grand slams, held in Queens.
Feast of St Gennaro: A 10-day festival based in Little Italy's Mulberry Street; stands dispense food and an image of the patron saint of Naples is showered with dollar bills.
Lincoln Center Out of Doors: Free performances of music, opera, dance and theater events on the plazas of Lincoln Center.

October *Columbus Day Parade:* Italians celebrate their heritage in a parade along Fifth Avenue.
Halloween Parade: Amazing costumes and masks worn in a parade through Greenwich Village.

November *New York Marathon:* Begins in Staten Island and concludes in Central Park.
Macy's Thanksgiving Day Parade: Massive balloons paraded along Central Park West and Broadway.

December Lighting of a tree at Rockefeller Center marks the start of the Christmas season.
New Year's Eve in Times Square: The ball drops and thousands dance in the streets.

Getting there

BY AIR

John F. Kennedy Airport

24km (15 miles) to city centre

- 60–100 minutes (subway)
- 45–65 minutes (Express Bus)
- 45–60 minutes

LaGuardia Airport

13km (8 miles) to city centre

- N/A
- 40–50 minutes
- 20–40 minutes

Newark Liberty International Airport

26km (16 miles) to city centre

- 30 minutes (AirTrain)
- 40–50 minutes (Express Bus)
- 35–50 minutes

New York has three main airports: John F. Kennedy Airport (tel: 718/244-4444), LaGuardia Airport (tel: 718/533-3400) and Newark Liberty International Airport (tel: 973/961-6000). International flights fly into John F. Kennedy and Newark airports and most domestic flights are handled by LaGuardia. All are part of the Port Authority of New York and New Jersey (www.panynj.gov). For driving and transit information, call Air Ride 800/247-7433 or visit the website.

John F. Kennedy International Airport has nine passenger terminals. Three are dedicated to specific carriers; British Airways operates from Terminal 7, JetBlue from Terminal 6 and Delta Airlines from Terminals 2 and 3. The remaining six terminals handle all the other major international carriers.

For transfers from the airport head to a Transportation Center booth where you will be able to make transport bookings and be given directions to public transit. Taxis from stands in front of the terminals charge a flat rate of $45 plus tolls—expensive for one person but not for two or three. When traveling back to the airport the fee is on the meter.

The AirTrain is an inexpensive way to travel and connects with the A and other subway routes. See www.panynj.gov for routes and schedules.

The SuperShuttle Manhattan is a shared-ride van service that operates 24 hours (tel: 212/315-3006 or 800/451-0455; www.supershuttle.com) and is moderately priced. The vans fill with passengers who are all headed to the same part of the city and serve the area between Battery Park and 125th Street (96th Street from Newark Airport). Reserve seats on a SuperShuttle at the Ground Transportation Center.

Alternatively, the New York Airport Service Express Bus (tel: 718/875-8200) operates a service that stops at Penn Station, the Port Authority Bus Terminal and Grand Central Terminal.

LaGuardia Airport is in Queens. Taxis charge metered rates, typically $24–$30 plus tolls. The SuperShuttle Manhattan and the New York Airport Service or Express Bus also operate from LaGuardia. Alternatively there are buses (take note: no luggage racks) that connect with the subway to take you to town; the Q47 and the Q33 connect with the 7 subway service, which stops at Grand Central Terminal and Times Square.

Newark International Airport is in New Jersey. Taxi transfers to Newark are expensive and will charge more to go to Upper East Side than to Midtown. The SuperShuttle Manhattan service also operates 24 hours from Newark. Another transfer option is Newark Liberty Airport Express Bus (tel: 877/863-9275; www.coachusa.com) an express bus which makes stops at Penn Station, the Port Authority and Grand Central Terminal. There is also an AirTrain which links the airport with Amtrak or the New Jersey commuter train. See the website www.panynj.gov for the schedule.

TRAIN AND BUS STATIONS

New York's long-distance train and bus terminals are located on the West Side.

For trains there are Grand Central Terminal, Park Avenue at 42nd Street, Metro North (tel: 212/532-4900) and Pennsylvanian Station, 7th Avenue between 31st and 33rd streets, where Long Island Railroad and New Jersey Transit trains stop and where you can connect with the subway system or catch a taxi.

For buses, go to the Port Authority Bus Terminal 8th Avenue between 40th and 42nd streets (tel: 212/564-8484), where buses from New Jersey and interstate and Canada serve the terminal.

Getting around

PUBLIC TRANSPORTATION

Public transit information is available 24 hours by phone (tel: 718/330-1234) or see the website www.mta.info. Buy multi-trip MetroCards at the entrance to the stations and swipe them through the turnstile to access the subway platform or bus. Schedules and maps are available from the concourse of Grand Central Terminal.

Trains The subway is the fastest way to travel around New York. The five principal services mainly run parallel routes along Manhattan's main avenues. PATH trains from Penn Station serve New Jersey and MTA trains from Grand Central Terminal serve towns north of the city.

Buses The bus system is simpler but slower than the subway, but has the advantage of cross-town routes. There are more than 200 bus routes, with stops every two or three blocks. Buses are equipped with lifts for wheelchair access.

Ferries The Staten Island Ferry (tel: 718/727-2508 or 311; www.siferry.com) runs a 24-hour service. Circle Line (tel: 212/563-3200; www.circleline42.com) sightseeing cruises run tours from Pier 83 at 42nd Street and 12th Avenue that circle Manhattan Island and from Battery Park to Ellis Island and the Statue of Liberty. Also from Pier 16 at South Street Seaport.

TAXIS

Yellow Cabs display an illuminated sign on the roof when available for hire, and can then be hailed on the street. There are a few taxi ranks at high-traffic areas such as Grand Central Terminal. Drivers are legally bound to take you anywhere within the five New York Boroughs but will charge for bridge or tunnel tolls.

Stretch limousines (with a driver) can also be booked at competitive rates if 8 to 10 people share.

DRIVING

Driving is not recommended in Manhattan. Parking places are costly and difficult to find. If you break down with a rented car, call the rental company, or the breakdown number which should be prominently displayed on or near the dashboard.

- There are no right turns on red lights within the New York City limits.
- Drive on the right.
- Speed limit on freeways: 55–65mph (88–105kph).
- Speed limit on main roads: 50–55mph (80–88kph).
- Speed limit on urban roads: 25–40mph (40–65kph), relevant to the area.
- Seat belts are compulsory for everyone in the front seats and for children in the back.
- Drivers can be stopped at random for a breathalyzer test (alcotest) by police. Zero tolerance is now the police code in New York.
- Gas (petrol) is sold in American gallons. Five American gallons equal 18 liters. Most late-night and 24-hour gas stations require you to pay the cashier before filling commences.

CAR RENTAL

There are many car rental companies and prices are competitive. You must be over 25 and have a credit card to rent a car. The main rental companies have toll-free (800) telephone numbers, and airports and hotel lobbies will provide details. Special weekend deals are widely available. A full valid E.U. driving license is acceptable, or an International Driving Permit.

FARES AND TICKETS

Public transportation Fares are a flat $2 for both subways and buses. There are discounts for seniors and people with disabilities, and children under 44 inches (1.13m) ride free. The easiest way to pay is by MetroCard, which can be topped up and gives you a free ride for every $10 spent. The $7 Fun Pass allows travel on buses (not express routes) and subways until 3am the next morning and is available from MetroCard vending machines and Times Square Visitor Center but not at subway station booths.

Attractions Most museums and attractions have discounts for seniors, students and children. New York CityPass and New York Pass, available at visitor centers, offer admission to several attractions at a discount.

Being there

NEW YORK CITY'S OFFICIAL VISITOR INFORMATION CENTER

www.nycvisit.com
810 Seventh Avenue
NY 10019

☎ 1-800/NYC-VISIT or
212/484-1222
City information ☎ 311

KIOSKS

Downtown
NYC Heritage Tourism Center
City Hall Park at Park Row
Chinatown
Canal/Walker/Baxter streets

Harlem
Nubian Heritage Center
2037 Fifth Avenue (between 125th
and 126th streets)

TIMES SQUARE INFORMATION CENTER

1560 Broadway between 46th and 47th streets. Operated by Times
Square Alliance, a nonprofit organization that offers a free walking tour
(tel: 212/768-1560; www.timessquarenyc.org). Open daily 8–8.

TKTS half-price ticket booths

Broadway and 47th Street and South Street Seaport's Pier 17 operated by
Theater Development Fund, a nonprofit organization (tel: 212/221-0885;
www.tdf.org).

MONEY

U.S. dollar traveler's checks and credit cards are accepted with photo ID
in most places (not taxis). Bills (notes) are 1, 5, 10, 20, 50 and 100 dollars.
One dollar is 100 cents. Coins are 1 cent (penny), 5 cents (nickel),
10 cents (dime), 25 cents (quarter) and 50 cents.

TIPS/GRATUITIES

Yes ✓ No ✗		
Restaurants (waiters, waitresses)	✓	15%
Hotels (chambermaids, doormen etc)	✓	$1
Bar service	✓	15%
Taxis	✓	15%
Porters	✓	$1 per bag

POSTAL AND INTERNET SERVICES

The main branch of the U.S. Post Office is on Manhattan's West Side, at 441 Eighth Avenue/33rd Street, NY 10001 (tel: 212/330-3002). Open 24 hours. Other post offices can be found in Yellow Pages. Most are open Mon–Fri 9–5, Sat 8–4. Mail boxes are on street corners. Hotel desks can provide many mail services.

Most hotels offer internet access. Kinko's has internet access in locations around the city, and many branches are open 24 hours (tel: 800/2-KINKOS). The Starbucks coffee shop chain also has wireless service. Internet cafés include Cybercafé, 250 W 49th Street at Broadway/Eighth Avenue (tel: 212/333-4109).

TELEPHONES

International dialling codes
Making overseas calls from hotel phones can be expensive. International phone cards can make calls more affordable. Dial 011 followed by UK: 44

Ireland: 353
Australia: 61
Germany: 49
Netherlands: 31

Emergency telephone numbers
Police, Fire, Ambulance: 911

EMBASSIES AND CONSULATES

UK ☎ 212/745 0200
Canada ☎ 212/596-1628
Germany ☎ 212/610-9700

Netherlands ☎ 877/388 2443
Spain ☎ 212/355-4080
Australia ☎ 212/351-8500

HEALTH ADVICE

Sun advice New York can be very hot and humid in summer. It is wise to use a sunscreen and drink plenty of fluids.
Drugs Pharmacies are on almost every block. If you need regular medication, take your own drugs and your prescription (for U.S. Customs). For after-hours emergencies several branches of Duane Reade are open 24 hours, including 224 W 57th Street/Broadway (tel: 212/541-9708).

Safe water Restaurants usually provide a glass of iced water. Drinking unboiled water from taps is safe. Mineral water is readily available.

PERSONAL SAFETY
Crime levels in New York have fallen sharply over recent years. But it is still wise to take sensible precautions:
- Do not ride the subway alone after midnight.
- Do not walk quiet streets or Central Park alone after dark.
- Carry only the cash you need, leave other cash and valuables in the hotel safe.
- Report theft or mugging to the nearest police station; this will provide a reference for your insurance company.

ELECTRICITY
The power supply is 110/120 volts AC (60 cycles). Sockets take two-prong, flat-pin plugs. Visitors should bring adapters for their 2-round-pin and 3-pin plugs. European visitors will need to bring either a dual voltage facility or a transformer.

OPENING HOURS

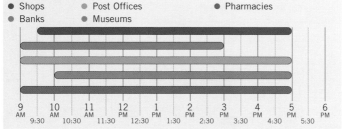

Shop hours vary greatly but generally open 9–10am until 5–6pm and many stay open later in the evening; some open Sunday noon–5. Some banks open until 3:30pm or 4pm. Post offices open Saturday until 1pm. There are more than 2,500 places of worship in New York of every religious denomination—see Yellow Pages for addresses and contact details. Opening times of museums vary, check with individual museums.

BEING THERE

LANGUAGE

The official language of the U.S.A. is English. New Yorkers are a mix of
cultures from all over the world and many different languages and dialects
are spoken. It helps if you can make yourself understood in English or
Spanish. Below are some words in common usage where they differ from
the English spoken in the U.K.

shop	*store*	trousers	*pants*
chemist (shop)	*drugstore*	nappy	*daiper*
cinema	*movie theater*	post	*mail*
pavement	*sidewalk*	post code	*zip code*
subway	*underpass*	ring up, telephone	*call*
toilet	*rest room*	autumn	*fall*
holiday	*vacation*	tap	*faucet*
fortnight	*two weeks*	suitcase	*case or bag*
ground floor	*first floor*	hotel porter	*bellhop*
first floor	*second floor*	chambermaid	*room maid*
flat	*apartment*	surname	*last name*
lift	*elevator*	cupboard	*closet*
1 cent coin	*penny*	banknote	*bill*
5 cent coin	*nickel*	dollar (colloquial)	*buck*
10 cent coin	*dime*	cashpoint	*ATM*
25 cent coin	*quarter*	bill (restaurant)	*check*
grilled	*broiled*	biscuit	*cookie*
frankfurter	*frank*	scone	*biscuit*
prawns	*shrimp*	sorbet	*sherbet*
aubergine	*eggplant*	jolly	*jello*
courgette	*zucchini*	jam	*jelly*
maize	*corn*	confectionery	*candy*
chips (potato)	*fries*	spirit	*liquor*
crisps (potato)	*chips*	soft drink	*soda*
railway	*railroad, railway*	single ticket	*one-way ticket*
underground	*subway*	return ticket	*round-trip ticket*

33

Best places to see

1 Central Park

www.centralparknyc.org

Central Park, a mighty rectangle of green, is the soothing bucolic heart of Manhattan.

Filling 843 acres (341ha), Central Park evolved during the late 19th century as the visionary plans of Frederick Olmsted and Calvert Vaux—intended to turn a collection of pig farms and squatters' camps into a "specimen of God's handiwork"—took shape. Creating glades and rock outcrops, the landscaping also involved the planting of more than 4 million trees and the digging of the sunken roads that render traffic crossing the park invisible. Fifth Avenue became a fashionable address as the millionaires of the day erected handsome park-view mansions along the eastern side and crossed the park in carrriages. For New York's poor, the park provided a much-needed escape from sweatshops and filthy tenements.

The park continues to mirror the full range of New York life. Whether jogging, rollerblading, strolling or walking the dog, Manhattanites of all kinds relish its green spaces—though in several isolated sections lone visitors can be vulnerable to crime. Pick up a park map from the Visitor Center in the Dairy (mid-park at 65th Street), built in 1870 and first used as a place where traditionally attired milkmaids dispensed milk to mothers and

babies, and plot a route to the numerous points of interest in the park.

Cross the Sheep Meadow (which once really did hold sheep) for the Lake and the Ramble or stroll through the Mall, a formally laid-out promenade that continues towards Bethesda Terrace. Among the more recent additions to the park is Strawberry Fields, laid out as a tribute to British musician John Lennon and overlooked by the Dakota Building where he lived and was fatally shot.

➕ C5 ✉ Between 59th and 110th streets, and Fifth Avenue and Central Park West ☎ 212/794-6564 or 800/201-7275 🕐 Always open; for safety, visit only during daylight ✋ Free 🍴 Tavern on the Green ($$$); snack stands 🚇 59th Street, 72nd Street, 81st Street, 96th Street, 103rd Street, 110th Street 🚌 1, 2, 3, 4, 5, 10, 30, 66, 72, 86, 104, Q32 ❓ Special events throughout the year

2 Chrysler Building

Even in a city packed with architecture of great merit, the Chrysler Building stands in a class of its own.

The definitive symbol of New York art deco and briefly the world's tallest building, the 1,048ft (320m) Chrysler Building was completed in 1930 and remains one of the most distinctive features on the Manhattan skyline. Reflecting the car manufacturing business of the building's owners and the era's enthusiasm for machine-inspired design, many features echo automobile design. Architect William Van Alen made the first large-scale use of stainless steel on a building exterior, employed hub caps as decoration on each setback and made the attention-grabbing spire resemble a car's radiator grille, complete with outward-leaping gargoyles.

Once partly used as a showroom for new Chrysler cars, the lobby underwent a

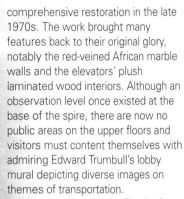

comprehensive restoration in the late 1970s. The work brought many features back to their original glory, notably the red-veined African marble walls and the elevators' plush laminated wood interiors. Although an observation level once existed at the base of the spire, there are now no public areas on the upper floors and visitors must content themselves with admiring Edward Trumbull's lobby mural depicting diverse images on themes of transportation.

The completion of the Empire State Building in 1931 robbed the Chrysler of its "world tallest" status, though the title was acquired in the first place only through some slightly devious behavior by Van Alen. The needle-like spire that tops the Chrysler Building's 77 stories was secretly assembled inside the tower and pushed through the roof. In doing so, Van Alen outwitted his former partner, H. Craig Severance, whose Bank of Manhattan Building (40 Wall Street), completed at just about the same time, would otherwise have earned the accolade.

✚ E11 ✉ 405 Lexington Avenue
☎ 212/682-3070
🕐 Mon–Fri 7am–6pm. Closed holidays
🎫 Free 🚇 Grand Central 🚌 42, 98, 101, 102, 104

3 Empire State Building

www.esbnyc.com

Perhaps not the best or even the best loved, but the Empire State Building is certainly the world's best-known New York skyscraper.

Conceived in the booming 1920s but built in the gloom of the Depression, the Empire State Building rose at a rate of four-and-a-half stories a week and was completed in just 410 days. By the time it was finished, however, the Wall Street Crash had left few companies able to afford its rents, despite the prestige of being housed in the world's tallest building, at a height of 1,454ft (442m) to the top

of its lightning rod. Through its early years, the building's only source of income came from visitors paying to enjoy the panorama of 80 miles (130km) from its 86th-floor observation level.

The building is a major sight among New York's art deco constructions. From a base filling 2 acres/1ha (the site of the original Astoria Hotel), the limestone and steel structure rises as a smooth-sided shaft with windows set flush with the wall. Inside, the three-story lobby boasts marble walls and aluminum decoration, including the panels added in the 1960s depicting the "eight" wonders of the world—the well-known seven plus the Empire State Building itself.

The building's 73 elevators include those designed to whisk sightseers to the observation levels at an astonishing rate of 1,200ft (365m) per minute, and can take just seconds from the lobby to the 80th floor. From there, two elevators lead up to the 86th floor, where there are outdoor promenades on all four sides of the building and a heated glassed-in area. There's also an observatory on the 102nd floor (additional fee). The slower and much more arduous route, by foot up 1,576 steps, is no longer open to the public, but is undertaken annually in the Empire Step-Up race, completed by the speediest competitors in less than 10 minutes.

✚ H14 ✉ 350 Fifth Avenue ☎ 212/736-3100 🕔 Daily 8am–2am 👍 Expensive 🍴 Snack bar ($) 🚇 34th Street 🚌 1, 2, 3, 4, 5, 6, 7, 16, 34, Q32 ❓ New York Skyride, a helicopter ride simulator on the second floor

4 Grand Central Terminal

www.grandcentralterminal.com

From an architectural viewpoint, there are few bigger, bolder or more beautiful places to buy a train ticket than Grand Central Terminal, built to house Cornelius Vanderbilt's railroad network in the early 20th century.

The halcyon years of American rail travel saw Grand Central Terminal labeled "the gateway to the nation" and a red carpet set along a platform for passengers boarding the evening service to Chicago. As if to cement the terminal's metaphorical place at the heart of the nation's life, its name was (inaccurately) used as the title of a popular radio soap opera, Grand Central Station, first broadcast in 1937. Now, it is mostly commuters to Connecticut's and New York's northern suburbs who can be found in lines at the ticket booths inside the Main Concourse.

Nearly demolished in 1968, the terminal was restored in the 1990s and now serves as the hub for dozens of shops and restaurants, including the Oyster Bar, which opened in 1913. The Main Concourse, 275ft by 120ft (84m by 37m), enjoys a *beaux arts* form and a staircase modeled on one in the Paris Opera. Above, the vaulted ceiling, 125ft (38m) high, is decorated by artist Paul Helleu's interpretation of the zodiac constellations. Although architects Warren and Wetmore take credit for the Main Concourse, much of the terminal's design is thought to be the work of another architectural firm, Reed and Stem.

The southern facade, clad in limestone and modeled on a Roman triumphal arch, features Jules Coutane's sculpture of Mercury supported by Minerva and Hercules.

✚ E11 ✉ 42nd Street and Lexington Avenue ◉ Daily 5:30am–1:30am ✋ Free 🍴 Various restaurants ($$–$$$), cafés and snack stands ($–$$) 🚇 Grand Central 🚌 1, 2, 3, 4, 5, 42, 98, 101, 102, 104, Q32 ❓ Guided tours Wed 12:30 from Information booth on Main Concourse ☎ 212/340-2345

5 Greenwich Village

The cafés, restaurants and bars of culturally vibrant Greenwich Village are a major element in Manhattan social life.

Created as a wealthy residential neighborhood in the 1780s, Greenwich Village then marked the northern extent of Manhattan's settlement and served to keep the rich away from the diseases sweeping through the poorer social strata to the south. As the rich moved on, their vacated brownstone townhouses became apartments for newly arrived migrants who swiftly established businesses. By the turn of the 20th century, the

Village was an ethnically diverse and socially tolerant area, with low rents that helped attract the creative and unconventional members of what was later lauded as the first American bohemia. Henry James, Eugene O'Neill and Edward Hopper were among the locally based novelists, dramatists and artists who created its cultural reputation. By the 1950s, Beat writers such as Allen Ginsberg and Jack Kerouac and abstract expressionist painters like Willem de Kooning were gathering in the area's cafés, and a decade later, the folk clubs that launched Bob Dylan.

Gentrification raised rents through the 1970s and 1980s and Greenwich Village people today are more likely to be successful lawyers or publishers than striving creative types. The haphazard streets are a delight to stroll, packed with unusual stores and lined by well-tended brownstones, many sporting "stoops" (entrance steps, a style introduced by 17th-century Dutch settlers that was used to prevent flooding back in the Netherlands) attractively decorated by their occupants.

At the heart of the action are New York University and Washington Square Park—a domain of skateboarders, buskers and onlookers, above which stands the triumphal Memorial Arch. Bordering the Village on the west is the Meatpacking District, now an area of trendy restaurants and nightlife.

➕ G18 ✉ Bordered by 14th Street, Hudson Street, Broadway and Houston Street 🚇 W 14th Street or Christopher Street 🚌 1, 2, 3, 5, 8, 10

6 Guggenheim Museum

www.guggenheim.org

The architecture might overpower the art but fans of both will find plenty to thrill them at this landmark museum.

Frank Lloyd Wright's stunningly designed Guggenheim Museum is a daring addition to the Fifth Avenue landscape. Outside, its curves and horizontally accentuated form is at odds with the traditional architecture all around, and inside, the

THE THANNHAUSER COLLEC

THE

exhibits are arranged along a spiral ramp where visitors start at the top and make their way down.

Solomon R. Guggenheim differed from other art investors by switching from Old Masters to invest his silver- and copper-mining wealth into the emerging European abstract scene of the 1920s. Guggenheim acquired works by the major exponents such as Léger and Gleizes, and a spectacular stash of paintings by Vasily Kandinsky. With these works and others hanging on the walls of his apartment at the stylish Plaza Hotel, Guggenheim set up a foundation in 1937 to promote public appreciation of abstract art that eventually grew into the present-day museum, which opened 10 years after Guggenheim's death, in 1959.

Selections from the Guggenheim collections, which range from Klee and Mondrian to Koons and Robert Mapplethorpe, are shown on rotation and share space with high-quality temporary exhibitions. A broader selection of art is displayed in the Thannhauser Tower, a 1992 addition with a permanent exhibit of the acquisitions of art collector and dealer Justin K. Thannhauser. These include important pieces by Gauguin, Picasso, Van Gogh, and Cézanne.

✚ D4 ✉ 1071 Fifth Avenue ☎ 212/423-3500
🕐 Sat–Wed 10–5:45, Fri 10–7:45. Closed Jan 1, Dec 25
💰 Expensive 🍴 Café ($–$$) 🚇 86th Street
🚌 1, 2, 3, 4, 18 ❓ Lectures

7 Metropolitan Museum of Art

www.metmuseum.org

Founded in 1870, this mighty museum is a vast collection of anything and everything of artistic value ever produced anywhere in the world.

More than deserving of its reputation as one of the world's greatest museums, the Met's contents exhaust visitors long before visitors exhaust them. Make use of the information center at ground level to plan your explorations and be selective. Special exhibitions are often crowded; go early on a weekday if you can. Art lovers can meander through galleries that chart virtually the entire course of Western art. The new, enlarged galleries for 19th- and early 20th-century European paintings hold a stunning collection of Impressionist and Post-Impressionist works, one of the largest such collections outside Paris, with noted works by Cézanne, Gauguin, Renoir, and Van Gogh.

The influential paintings of the Hudson River School and a series of period-furnished rooms highlight the increasing self-assurance of American art as the country evolved into an independent nation. Among the strong points are a dazzling

stock of Tiffany glasswork and a special section devoted to architect Frank Lloyd Wright.

With 36,000 objects from pre-dynastic times to the arrival of the Romans, the Ancient Egyptian section begins with a walk-through reconstruction of the Tomb of Perneb and continues with cases of immaculately preserved original exhibits. Major assemblages of Roman and Greek art, Chinese and Japanese ceramics, medieval European art (which continues at the Cloisters, ➤ 108), European arms and armor, the art of Africa, Oceania and the Americas, musical instruments, plus galleries of drawings, prints and photography, and modern art, consume only some of the rest of this museum. The galleries of Islamic art are closed for renovation, but a selection of exquisite objects is on display.

✚ D5 ✉ 1000 Fifth Avenue ☎ 212/535-7710 🕐 Tue–Thu and Sun 9:30–5:15, Fri and Sat 9:30–8:45 💷 Expensive 🍴 Restaurant ($$), cafeteria and cafés ($) 🚇 86th Street 🚌 1, 2, 3, 4, 18 (includes admission to the Cloisters on same day) ❓ Lectures, films

8 Museum of Modern Art

www.moma.org

Probably the world's best repository of modern painting and an excellent exhibitor of sculpture, film, and video.

It is hard to believe today, but when the Museum of Modern Art (MoMA, as it is known) staged its first exhibition in 1929 the featured artists—Cézanne, Van Gogh, Gauguin and Seurat—were not represented anywhere else in the city and were considered too risky by the Met. Despite this, 47,000 people attended the exhibition over four months and, a decade later, the museum acquired its current site, a gift from the wealthy Rockefeller family.

As the new museum was being created, the outbreak of war in Europe caused many leading artists to leave Paris for New York, making the city the center of the art world and setting the scene for abstract expressionism, the U.S.'s first internationally influential art movement.

Abstract expressionism accounts for some of the most noted holdings: Pollock's immense and spellbinding *One*, Rothko's shimmering blocks of color, and works by De Kooning. European contributions include Van Gogh's much eulogized *Starry Night*, one of Monet's *Water Lilies*, Matisse's *Dance*, Picasso's *Three Women at the Spring*, Braque's *Man With A*

Guitar, and Mondrian's *Broadway Boogie-Woogie* revealing the impact of New York's jazz rhythms and grid-style streets on the Dutch artist.

A soaring remodeled building designed by Yoshio Taniguchi opened in 2004 with nearly twice the space. It preserves Philip Johnson's 1953 design of the beloved Abby Aldrich Rockefeller Sculpture Garden and allows works to be displayed in new juxtapositions. The most modern pieces are displayed on the second floor, with selections from the permanent collection on the fourth and fifth floors. That collection also includes some 22,000 films and videos, and there's a regular program of screenings. The department devoted to architecture and design includes the Mies van der Rohe archive and an eclectic range of objects.

✚ D9 ✉ 11 W 53rd Street
☎ 212/708-9400 🕐 Sat–Mon, Wed–Thu 10:30–5:30, Fri 10:30–8
💰 Expensive (free Fri 4–8)
🍴 Restaurant ($$$) and cafés ($–$$)
🚇 Fifth Avenue, 53rd Street 🚌 1, 2, 3, 4, 5 ❓ Films, lectures

9 Statue of Liberty

www.nps.gov/stli

The most potent and enduring symbol of the U.S. as the land of opportunity is the landmark Statue of Liberty.

Nowadays it is strange to think that an American emblem known worldwide was initially intended by its creator, Frenchman Frédéric-August Bartholdi, to stand in Egypt above the Suez Canal. The plans were rejected, but in 1871 on a visit to New York, the sculptor found the perfect site for his torch-carrying lady—at the entrance to the city's harbor. Equally surprising in retrospect is the antipathy towards the project on the American side following the decision for costs to be shared between France and the U.S. as a sign of friendship and shared democratic ideals.

As the lady, formally titled *Liberty Enlightening the World*, took shape in Bartholdi's Paris studio, the pedestal—the responsibility of the U.S.—made slow progress due to lack of funds, which prompted newspaper publisher Joseph Pulitzer to mount a campaign to raise money through small donations. The finished statue arrived in New York in June 1885 and Pulitzer announced that $100,000 had been collected. The lady was placed atop the pedestal and dedicated in October 1886.

Ferries to the statue, which is 152ft (46m) high, leave regularly from Battery Park, also stopping at Ellis Island. Access is limited, so order tickets in advance. Once ashore, visitors not only have an excellent view of the lower Manhattan skyline but can tour the Statue of Liberty museum on the 16-story-high pedestal level. Exhibits document the history and symbolism of the statue, while the interior of the statue itself can be glimpsed through a glass ceiling. Further access is not possible.

✚ J24 (off map) ✉ Liberty Island ☎ 212/269-5755 (ferry information); 212/363-3200 (statue information) 🕐 Daily 9:30–5 (extended hours in peak season) ✋ Free; ferry expensive 🍴 Cafeteria ($) 🚢 Battery Park ❓ Tours

10 Times Square

www. TimesSquarenyc.org

If a single spot yells "this is New York" to the world at large, it is Times Square with its towering, animated neon signs.

A gathering place for hundreds of thousands celebrating each New Year's Eve and the heart of New York's theater district, Times Square is a frenetic, gaudy and until the late 1990s, rather seedy intersection whose fame far outstrips its actual appeal. The immediate area fell into social decline after World War II, but a major campaign to rid the area of its prostitutes, drug dealers and street con artists, and to limit the numbers of porno cinemas and adult bookshops in its vicinity, met with considerable success.

Designated a Business Improvement District under a nationwide plan financed by a tax on local businesses, the square steadily became safe for tourists and legitimate businesses with a major new development of hotels, shopping complexes, and office blocks, and the restoration of many historic theaters. Major retail franchises, a number of theme restaurants, and a never-ending stream of sightseers now dominate the area, which is patroled by an unarmed security force.

Times Square was originally Longacre Square, but acquired a new name in 1904 when the owner of the *New York Times* got permission to build the office tower (One Times Square) from which the

New Year's ball is still dropped. By the 1920s, the vibrant New York theater district had become established on nearby streets. Erected in the heyday of vaudeville, many of the plush theaters remain in varied states of restoration. Through the 1930s, the local section of Broadway became known as "the Great White Way" for its immense electrically lit marquees and advertising billboards.

✚ C11 ✉ Between Broadway and Seventh Avenue, 42nd and 47th streets 🚇 Times Square 🚌 5, 6, 7, 10, 42, 104 ❓ Walking tours

Best things to do

Good places to have lunch

▼▼▼ Fleur de Sel ($$$)

A lunchtime tasting menu shows off the distinctive approach to French cuisine.

✉ 5 E 20th Street ☎ 212/460-9100

▼▼ ▼▼ Gotham Bar and Grill ($$$)

See page 60.

Grand Central Oyster Bar ($–$$)

Feast on seafood at the counter or beneath the tiled arches of the dining room, as commuters have done for nearly a century.

✉ Grand Central Terminal, lower level ☎ 212/490-6650; www.oysterbarny.com 🕔 Closed Sun

🔻🔻🔻 Katz's Deli ($)

Harry met Sally at this Lower East Side landmark. Come here for the pastrami, the knishes and a classic New York experience.

✉ 205 East Houston Street ☎ 212/254-2246; www.katzdeli.com

Mandarin Court ($)

This is the perfect place to stop for dim sum.

✉ 61 Mott Street, Chinatown ☎ 212/608-3838

🔻🔻 Mars 2112 ($$)

Futuristic theme restaurant in the heart of Manhattan near Times Square.

✉ Corner of 51st Street and Broadway ☎ 212/582-2112

Suzie's ($)

Chinese eatery popular for its well-priced lunch specials.

✉ 163 Bleecker Street, Greenwich Village ☎ 212/777-1395

🔻🔻🔻 Tabla ($$)

Come here for a modern take on Indian food.

✉ 11 Madison Avenue ☎ 212/889-0667

🔻🔻🔻 Victor's Café ($$–$$$)

Cuban cuisine; vibrant atmosphere.

✉ 236 W 52nd Street, Midtown Manhattan
☎ 212/586-7714

Excellent restaurants

Alouette ($$)
A simple bistro serving classic fare, beautifully presented and reasonably priced.
✉ 2588 Broadway ☎ 212/222-6808 🕐 Dinner 🚇 96th Street

♦♦ Babbo ($$$)
Chef Mario Batali creates original Italian dishes at his flagship restaurant. An excellent wine list compliments the superb food.
✉ 110 Waverly Place between 6th Avenue and MacDougal Street
☎ 212/777-0303; www.babbonyc.com 🕐 Dinner

Bottino ($$–$$$)
Among the trendiest eateries in increasingly trendy Chelsea. The garden offers a romantic dinner setting.
✉ 246 Tenth Avenue ☎ 212/206-6766; www.bottinonyc.com 🕐 Lunch Tue–Sat and dinner 🚇 23rd Street

♦♦ Daniel ($$$)
Immensely popular for high-quality French cuisine from Daniel Boulud, one of the city's leading chefs.
✉ 60 E 65th Street ☎ 212/288-0033; www.danielnyc.com 🕐 Dinner Mon–Sat 🚇 68th Street

♦♦ Four Seasons ($$$)
Inside the landmark Seagram Building and consistently rated as one of the best upscale dining experiences in New York.
✉ 99 E 52nd Street ☎ 212/754-9494; www.fourseasonsrestaurant.com
🕐 Lunch Mon–Fri, dinner Mon–Sat 🚇 51st Street

♦♦ Gotham Bar and Grill ($$$)
Reserve early for dinner at this shrine to New American cuisine, where rack of lamb is Alfred Portale's signature dish.
✉ 12 E 12th Street ☎ 212/620-4020; www.gothambarandgrill.com
🕐 Lunch and dinner 🚇 14th Street–Union Square

💎💎💎 Jean Georges ($$$)

Top French chef Jean Georges Vongerichten creates tastes for the
sophisticated palate at this restaurant overlooking Central Park.
✉ Trump International Hotel, 1 Central Park West between 60th and 61st
streets ☎ 212/299-3900; www.jean-georges.com 🕐 Lunch Mon–Fri, dinner
Mon–Sat 🚇 59th Street–Columbus Circle

💎💎 John's Pizzeria ($$)

John's thin crusts defined New York pizza from their Village base.
✉ 260 W 44th Street ☎ 212/391-7560; www.johnspizzerianyc.com
🕐 Lunch and dinner 🚇 42nd Street

💎💎 Nam ($$$)

This hip TriBeCa Vietnamese restaurant serves delicious main
courses such as chicken sauteed with lemongrass.
✉ 110 Reade Street ☎ 212/267-1777 🕐 Lunch Mon–Fri, dinner daily
🚇 Chambers Street

💎💎💎 Nobu ($$$)

Reserve your table well in advance to enjoy inventive, Japanese
cuisine created by chef Nobu Matsuhisa.
✉ 105 Hudson Street ☎ 212/219-0500; www.myriadrestaurantgroup.com
🕐 Lunch Mon–Fri, dinner daily 🚇 Franklin Street

Best museums

- American Museum of Natural History (▶ 106)

- Brooklyn Museum of Art (▶ 171)

- Cooper-Hewitt National Design Museum (▶ 110–111)

- Frick Collection
(► 114)

- Guggenheim
Museum
(► 46–47)

- Metropolitan
Museum of Art
(► 48–49)

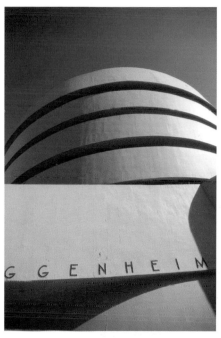

- Museum of Arts and Design (► 89)

- Museum of Modern Art (MoMA)
(► 50–51)

- New Museum of Contemporary Art
(► 155)

- Whitney Museum of American Art
(► 120)

Best views

- Lower Manhattan from the Brooklyn Bridge (➤ 148–149)

- Upper Manhattan and the Palisades from Fort Tryon Park

- Lower Manhattan from the Staten Island ferry

- The Chrysler Building from the observation level of the Empire State Building (➤ 40–41)

● Manhattan from Roosevelt Island (➤ 93)

● The modernist United Nations Buildings from the United Nations Plaza on First Avenue (➤ 97)

● Central Park from the observation deck at the Top of the Rock in the Rockefeller Center (➤ 92)

Places to take the children

American Museum of Natural History
The huge dinosaur structures here are sure to turn young heads; the adjacent Hayden Planetarium is another favorite (➤ 106).
www.amnh.org
✉ Central Park West at 79th Street ☎ 212/769-5100 ⏰ Daily 10–5:45 💷 Expensive 🚇 79th Street or 81st Street

Bronx Zoo
The largest zoo in the U.S. will easily keep youngsters amused for a whole day (➤ 169).
www.bronxzoo.com
✉ Bronx River Parkway and Fordham Road ☎ 718/367-1010
🚇 Pelham Parkway

Brooklyn Children's Museum
Since 1899 this museum has entertained and educated youngsters inside an architecturally innovative structure.
www.brooklynkids.org
✉ 145 Brooklyn Avenue, Brooklyn ☎ 718/735-4400
🚇 Kingston Avenue

Central Park Carousel
This restored vintage carousel is one of the most kid-pleasing attractions in New York.
www.centralparknyc.org
✉ Central Park, just south of 65th Street Transverse
🚇 59th Street–Columbus Circle

Charles A. Dana Discovery Center
On the northern edge of Central Park with engaging exhibits exploring environmental themes, and special events such as birdwatching for beginners and an artist-led walk through the park.

www.centralparknyc.org

✉ 110th Street and Fifth Avenue ☎ 212/860-1370 🚇 110th Street

Chelsea Piers Lanes

Ten-pin bowling raised to fine art and with bumper bowling for younger kids. At night "extreme bowling" comes with music, fog machines, laser lights and Day-Glo pins.

www.chelseapiers.com

✉ Between piers 59 and 60, west end of 23rd Street ☎ 212/835-2695
🚇 23rd Street

Children's Museum of the Arts

Hands-on art projects allow budding young Picassos to perfect their skills, inspired by rotating exhibitions of children's art from around the world. This family-oriented museum provides a playful balance to New York's major art museums.

www.cmany.org

✉ 182 Lafayette Street, between Broome and Grand ☎ 212/274-0986
🚇 Spring Street or Prince Street

FAO Schwarz

Possibly the world's most famous toy store, packed from floor to ceiling with the kind of toys most children can only dream about.

www.FAO.com

✉ 707 Fifth Avenue ☎ 212/044 9400 🚇 Fifth Avenue

New York SkyRide

After ascending to the observation levels of the Empire State Building (➤ 40–41), visit the independent New York SkyRide on the second floor where participants are given a virtual aerial tour of the city at dizzying speed aboard a "spacecoptor."

www.skyride.com

☎ 1-888/SKYRIDE or 212/279-9777

Top activities

Museums: There are many, and several are absolutely the world's best; allow ample time.

River: Take a sightseeing cruise.

Walk: Most New York neighborhoods are best explored on foot; bring sensible shoes.

Theater: Probably the best in the world; look up listings in the newspaper and choose a show that appeals.

Sit: On a park bench eating a knish or a bagel with cream cheese.

Architecture: From Federal Period to Post Modern, New York has got the lot. Buy an architecture specialty guide and choose your favorites.

Art: The old stuff is in the museums but the galleries of Chelsea showcase tomorrow's hot names.

Eat: A different ethnic dinner every evening.

Shop: Top designers, department stores, discounts outlets and second-hand bargains all are available here.

TV: Get a free ticket for the taping of a national show; find out how at the Convention and Visitors Bureau ("Things to Do" at www.nycvisit.com).

around
Midtown Manhattan

**Bisected by prestigious Fifth Avenue, in many ways
this is the heart of New York City.**

Start in Times Square.

Long a vibrant part of Midtown Manhattan, Times Square
(► 54–55) and its immediate area have been transformed
for the better in recent years. The completion of the former
New York Times building on the south side in 1904 gave the
square its name.

Walk north on Broadway and turn right onto 44th Street.

The Millennium Broadway, number 145 W, is among the
many new luxury hotels to appear in the area; filling a whole
block the lobby provides pedestrian access to 45th Street.

*Continue east along 44th Street to the Vanderbilt Avenue
entrance of Grand Central Terminal (► 42–43).*

Go into the terminal and up the long escalator to the left
and walk through the Met Life Building (► 88). Exit and
cross 45th Street and walk through the ornate Helmsley
Building to Park Avenue.

Walk north along Park Avenue.

On the right at 49th Street is the Waldorf-Astoria hotel
(► 79), renowned for pampering heads of state and other
notables since the 1930s. The art deco features of the
lobby merit a look. St. Bartholomew's Church, on the right,
between 50th and 51st streets, was completed in 1919 by

the celebrated New York architectural firm of McKim, Mead and White.

Walk two blocks west along 50th Street to Fifth Avenue.

Its main entrance facing Fifth Avenue, St. Patrick's Cathedral (➤ 94) was completed in 1879 in modified French Gothic style. Inside, the chapels and shrines glow in candlelight.

Turn left on Fifth Avenue, and cross at the Promenade. Head west into Rockefeller Plaza by the statue of Prometheus toward the skating rink (winter only). The GE Building is straight ahead, in the heart of the Rockefeller Center (➤ 92).

Distance 2–3 miles (3–5km)
Time 2–4 hours
Start point Times Square ✚ C11
End point Rockefeller Center ✚ D10
Lunch John's Pizzeria (➤ 61)

Classical music and performing arts

BAM
The Brooklyn Academy of Music specializes in major new works across the musical spectrum.
✉ 30 Lafayette Avenue ☎ 718/636-4100; www.bam.org
Ⓜ Lafayette Avenue

Carnegie Hall
Hear the world's top orchestras at this truly memorable venue.
✉ Corner 57th Street and Seventh Avenue ☎ 212/247-7800;
www.carnegiehall.org Ⓜ Seventh Avenue or 57th Street

Film Forum
One of New York's leading movie houses for independent movies and art films.
✉ 209 West Houston Street ☎ 212/727-8110; www.filmforum.org
Ⓜ West 4th Street or Houston Street

Jazz at Lincoln Center
This is the first facility ever created just for jazz. The Ertegun Jazz Hall traces the history of jazz.
✉ Time Warner Center at Broadway and West 60th Street ☎ 212/721-6500;
www.jalc.org Ⓜ 59th Street–Columbus Circle

Joan Weill Center
This architecturally stunning and largest dance-specific building in the U.S. is the home of the Alvin Ailey American Dance Theater.
✉ Corner 55th Street and Ninth Avenue ☎ 212/405-9000
Ⓜ 59th Street–Columbus Circle

Metropolitan Opera House
The Met's October opening night is a major New York occasion on the social calendar and the season continues until April.

✉ Lincoln Center, Columbus and 63rd Street ☎ 212/362-6000;
www.metopera.org 🚇 66th Street–Lincoln Center

New York City Ballet

The season for this renowned company runs from November to
December and from April to June.

✉ New York State Theater, Lincoln Center Plaza, Columbus and 63rd Street
☎ 212/870-5570; www.nycballet.com 🚇 66th Street–Lincoln Center

New York City Opera

This company offers newer works, operetta and some musicals.

✉ Lincoln Center, Columbus and 63rd Street ☎ 212/870-5570;
www.nycopera.com 🚇 66th Street–Lincoln Center

New York Philharmonic

Performances from mid-September to early June, as well as a
series of free summer recitals in each of the city's five boroughs.

✉ Avery Fisher Hall, Lincoln Center ☎ 212/875-5656;
www.newyorkphilharmonic.org 🚇 66th Street

Nightclubs

40/40 Club

Jay-z's two-level sophisticated sports bar blasts R&B and hip hop after the game.

West 25th Street ☎ 212/832-4040; www.the4040club.com
23rd Street

Baktun

Multimedia lounge for the discerning fans of house, drum'n'bass, and other electronic-based beats.

418 W 14th Street ☎ 212/206-1590; www.baktun.com
Closed Tue 14th Street/Eighth Avenue

Club Shelter

Warehouse-like space and lots of dancing to house music at this alcohol-free venue.

20 W 39th Street ☎ 212/719-4479; www.clubshelter.com
42nd Street

Columbus 72

Steamy, smartly dressed Latin disco on Tuesday and Saturday nights, as well as top 40s and classics on Saturdays, from the crowd at the legendary Copacabana nightclub.

246A Columbus Avenue, between 71st and 72nd streets
☎ 212/769-1492; www.copacabanany.com 72nd Street

Element

With a huge, hardwood dance floor and powerful sound system cranking out everything from reggae to disco and soul, this is one of the city's best dance clubs (Thursday to Sunday).

225 East Houston Street at Essex ☎ 212/254-2200;
www.elementny.com Lower East Side–Second Avenue

Sapphire Lounge

Small by club standards, the Sapphire Lounge is a long-time survivor and pioneer of the nightclub invasion of the Lower East Side. The place throbs to house, hip hop and rhythm and blues most nights.

✉ 249 Eldridge Street ☎ 212/777-5153; www.sapphirenyc.com 🚇 Second Avenue

SOBs

The name stands for Sounds of Brazil and that, plus similarly infectious rhythms from Africa and the Caribbean, is exactly what is delivered to an eager, stylish crowd ready to dance the night away.

✉ 204 Varick Street ☎ 212/243-4940; www.sobs.com 🚇 Houston Street

Sullivan Room

This small late-night basement club is a must for fans of techno and house music, played by some of the city's best DJs.

✉ 218 Sullivan Street ☎ 212/252-2151; www.sullivanroom.com 🚇 4th Street

Webster Hall

Lively and spacious venue with contrasting sounds in myriad rooms on four floors, and different themes each night.

✉ 125 E 11th Street ☎ 212/353-1600; www.websterhall.com 🚇 14th Street–Union Square

Bars

The Big Easy
A New Orleans theme bar on the Upper East Side.
✉ 1768 Second Avenue ☎ 212/348-0879 🚇 96th Street

Chumley's
Once a prohibition-era speakeasy; extensive bar range and the walls are lined with pictures of famous ex-regulars.
✉ 86 Bedford Street ☎ 212/675-4449 🚇 Christopher Street

d.b.a.
Popular hangout for East Village arty types with minimalist decor and more than 150 varieties of beer and many malt scotches.
✉ 41 First Avenue ☎ 212/475-5097; www.drinkgoodstuff.com
🚇 Second Avenue

Heartland
Big, brash, and often rowdy, but Heartland has a tremendous stash of beers it brews itself. Five Manhattan locations.

✉ 35 Union Square West ☎ 212/645-3400; www.heartandbrewery.com
🚇 14th Street–Union Square

Hudson Bar

Expensive martinis and more are served at New York's swankiest bar, amid the Philippe Starck decor of the trendy Hudson Hotel.
✉ 356 W 58th Street ☎ 212/554-6217; www.hudsonhotel.com
🚇 59th Street

McSorley's Old Ale House

Smoke-stained wood panels and photos of old New York all add to the atmosphere of one of the city's longest-serving bars.
✉ 15 E 7th Street ☎ 212/473-9148 🚇 Astor Place

Pete's Tavern

This traditional watering hole, two blocks from Gramercy Park, dates from 1864 and inspired O. Henry to write *The Gift of the Magi* within its walls.
✉ 129 East 18th Street at Irving Place ☎ 212/473-7676
🚇 14th Street–Union Square

Top of the Tower

With the East River on one side and Midtown Manhattan on the other, few public places have the choice New York views you'll get at this elegant art deco hotel bar.
🏨 Bookman Hotel, 3 Mitchell Place ☎ 212/980-4796 🚇 51st Street

White Horse Tavern

Welsh writer Dylan Thomas is supposed to have drunk his last here in this attractive Village pub frequented by locals, university students and tourists.
✉ 567 Hudson Street ☎ 212/243-9260 🚇 Christopher Street

Places to stay

▽▽▽▽ Affinia Gardens Hotel ($$$)

There is a quiet atmosphere in this small hotel (formerly the Lyden Garden). Spacious suites have fully equipped kitchens, and separate living areas with big TVs.

✉ 215 E 64th Street ☎ 212/355-1230; www.affinia.com 🚇 68th Street

▽▽▽ Carlyle ($$$)

The public rooms of this art deco building have crystal chandeliers, the private rooms are sumptuous and the service is impeccable.

✉ 35 E 76th Street ☎ 212/744-1600; www.thecarlyle.com 🚇 77th Street

▽▽ Edison ($–$$)

Not only an affordable choice for the Times Square area but also a delight for art deco fans, this large hotel has a friendly ambience.

✉ 228 W 47th Street ☎ 212/840-5000; www.edisonhotelnyc.com 🚇 50th Street

▽▽▽▽ Four Seasons ($$$)

Designed by I.M. Pei, the Four Seasons is among the most opulent of the New York hotels.

✉ 57 E 57th Street ☎ 212/758-5700; www.fourseasons.com 🚇 59th Street

▽▽ Franklin ($$)

The stylish Franklin suits those who prefer a smaller hotel. It is well placed for the Museum Mile on the Upper East Side.

✉ 164 E 87th Street ☎ 212/369-1000; www.franklinhotel.com 🚇 86th Street

▽▽▽▽ Le Parker Meridien ($$$)

The 730 bedrooms and suites in this sleek French hotel come complete with a CD/DVD player, 32-inch TV, desk, and chair.

✉ 118 W 57th Street ☎ 212/245-5000; www.parkermeridien.com 🚇 57th Street

▼▼▼ The Lucerne ($$–$$$)

The 200-plus bedrooms and suites are spacious and have marble bathrooms. The suites have a sitting area, some with a kitchenette with microwave and refrigerator.

✉ 201 W 79th Street ☎ 212/875-1000; www.thelucernehotel.com
🚇 79th Street

▼▼▼▼ Ritz-Carlton New York, Central Park ($$$)

This opulent hotel offers wonderful views, and telescopes for birdwatching are provided in rooms overlooking Central Park. The in-hotel restaurant is French.

✉ 50 Central Park South ☎ 212/308-9100; www.ritzcarlton.com
🚇 59th Street/Fifth Avenue

▼▼▼ SoHo Grand ($$$)

One of the first hotels to bring Midtown Manhattan levels of comfort and service to the chic confines of SoHo, its stylish bar and eatery still draw neighborhood celebrities.

✉ 310 W Broadway ☎ 212/965-3000 or 1-800/965-3000;
www.sohogrand.com 🚇 Canal Street

▼▼▼▼ Waldorf-Astoria ($$$)

A sightseeing stop for its opulent art deco lobby and place in New York history for accommodating royals and heads of state. This sumptuous 1931 landmark hotel features traditionally styled rooms and suites—1,246 of them—along with four restaurants, four bars and gym and spa facilities.

✉ 301 Park Avenue ☎ 212/355-3000;
www.waldorfastoria.com 🚇 51st Street

Best shopping

Barney's New York

Upper East Side old guard and downtown fashionistas alike shop here for international designers, make-up and accessories.

✉ 660 Madison Avenue ☎ 212/826-8900; www.barneys.com
Ⓜ 59th Street–Lexington Avenue

Bergdorf Goodman

When money is no object, New Yorkers come to this former Vanderbilt mansion to buy Armani and Vera Wang creations beneath crystal chandeliers and be fussed over by attentive, professional staff. Bergdorf Men is directly across Fifth Avenue.

✉ 754 Fifth Avenue ☎ 212/753-7300;
www.bergdorfgoodman.com Ⓜ 59th Street

FAO Schwarz

See page 67.

Jeffrey New York

Less pretentious than its Midtown counterparts and without the tourist bustle in its airy warehouse setting, Jeffrey's offers a great range of designer clothing for men and women and gains plaudits aplenty for its quality footwear.

✉ 449 W 14th Street ☎ 212/206-1272 Ⓜ 14th Street

Lord and Taylor

This lovely, somewhat old-fashioned store is particularly good for shirts, sweaters, trousers, and skirts, many sold under its own labels. The holiday windows, featuring animated figures, are a delight.

✉ 424 Fifth Avenue ☎ 212/391-3344; lordandtaylor.com
Ⓜ Grand Central

Macy's

With seven floors of selling space, Macy's claim to be the largest department store in the world is entirely believable. Shoppers can sift through kitchenware, cosmetics, clothing, footwear, stop for lunch and a haircut, and even buy a souvenir from the Metropolitan Museum of Art. Sales run all the time.

✉ 151 W 34th Street
☎ 212/695-4400;
www.macys.com 🚇 34th Street

Manhattan Mall

Across from Macy's this urban version of the all-American shopping mall has more than 50 stores offering fashion, household, gifts, electronics, food, and more.

✉ Sixth Avenue and 33rd Street ☎ 212/465-0500; www.manhattanmallny.com 🚇 34th Street Herald Square

Sak's Fifth Avenue

Top-notch clothing, linens and cosmetics for those who value quality and established designers. Known for its good service and beautiful holiday windows.

✉ 611 Fifth Avenue ☎ 212/753-4000; www.saksfifthavenue.com 🚇 Fifth Avenue

Takashimaya

Expect to pay high prices for beautiful things at this elegant, small branch of the Japanese emporium.

✉ 693 Fifth Avenue ☎ 212/350-0100; www.ny-takashimaya.com (Japanese) 🚇 Fifth Avenue

Exploring

Manhattan may only be a part of New York City, but as far as the world is concerned Manhattan is New York. For visitors from near and far, this long slender island is everything they ever imagined New York to be. Times Square, Broadway, Central Park, the Empire State Building, the Museum of Modern Art, and everything else that defines New York to the world at large has a Manhattan address and entices visitors to spend day after day tramping its streets with a sense of wonder.

Once acclimatized to the cruising yellow cabs, the street food vendors, legions of office workers crossing the road as one and the general commotion that fills many a Manhattan street, newcomers will find themselves steadily discovering another Manhattan: one of neighborhoods with a village-like insularity harboring undiscovered attractions on quiet residential streets.

Midtown Manhattan

With its skyscrapers, department stores, high-class hotels, hot-dog vendors, bustling office workers and tourists, Midtown Manhattan is for many visitors what New York is all about. From Times Square to glossy Fifth Avenue you will encounter crowds of sightseers as well as busy New Yorkers rushing to work while grabbing a hot dog "to go" and talking into a cell phone.

Franklin D Roosevelt Island

MIDTOWN MANHATTAN

BROADWAY

While the streets are teeming with humanity by day, after the evening rush hour much of the area is remarkably empty, save for areas such as the theater district around Times Square. Some of the city's best loved attractions lie between 8th Avenue and Lexington Avenue, with Fifth Avenue slicing through the middle to define the east and west.

The only deviation from Midtown's grid-style street layout is the

former Native American trail better known as Broadway, which cuts a diagonal path not only through Midtown Manhattan but continues 140 miles (225km) to the state capital, Albany.

CARNEGIE HALL

Carnegie Hall was built with $2 million from the fortune of industrialist Andrew Carnegie and has been highly regarded ever since Tchaikovsky arrived from Russia to conduct on the opening night in 1891. Guided tours lead visitors around the horseshoe-shaped auditorium, with world-famous acoustics, its design modeled on an Italian opera house.

The adjoining museum remembers many of the great artists who have appeared here.

www.carnegiehall.org

🕀 C9 ✉ 57th Street and 7th Avenue ☎ 212/247-7800 🕓 Other than shows, interior only on guided tours 🖐 Moderate; museum free
🚇 57th Street–7th Avenue ❓ Guided tours during the season
☎ 212/903 9765

CHRYSLER BUILDING

Best places to see, ➤ 38–39.

DAILY NEWS BUILDING

Easy to imagine as the home of the *Daily Planet* and mild-mannered Clark Kent, alter ego of Superman, the Daily News Building was the base of the newspaper of the same name until 1995. In the lobby is an immense globe. The architect of the art deco building was Raymond Hood, also the designer of the GE Building in Rockefeller Center.

➕ F11 ✉ 220 E 42nd Street 🕐 Lobby always open ✋ Free 🚇 42nd Street–Grand Central

GRAND CENTRAL TERMINAL

Best places to see, ➤ 42–43.

INTREPID SEA-AIR-SPACE MUSEUM

Seeing service in World War II and the Vietnam conflict, the aircraft carrier U.S.S. *Intrepid* is now spending its retirement years as a museum. The workings and wartime exploits of the vessel itself are comprehensively detailed, and the many exhibits arranged around its decks explore the changing face of warfare and document the technological innovations spawned by it.

A former British Airways Concorde is among the civilian aviation exhibits. Temporary exhibitions cover related themes. The museum reopened in November 2008, following a period of renovation.

www.intrepidmuseum.org

➕ A10 ✉ Pier 86, W 46th Street ☎ 212/245-0072
🕐 Call for opening times ✋ Expensive 🍴 Café ($) 🚇 42nd Street

LIPSTICK BUILDING

In a city that sometimes seems built entirely of towering rectangular blocks, the so-called Lipstick building dares to be different. Its nickname is earned by its elliptical shape, its telescoping tiers, and by its predominant colors of red, brown and pink. One of many buildings contributed to the New York skyline by veteran architect Philip Johnson and partner John Burgee, the Lipstick was completed in 1986.

➕ E9 ✉ 885 Third Avenue 🕐 Lobby always open ✋ Free 🍴 Café ($$)
🚇 Lexington–Third Avenue

MET LIFE BUILDING

Looming high above Grand Central Terminal and infamously blocking the view along Park Avenue, the Met Life Building (formerly the Pan Am Building) was completed in 1963 and became the largest commercial building in the world, rising 59 stories and offering 2.4 million sq ft (223,000sq m) of office space. Bauhaus mastermind Walter Gropius was among the architects that created the structure which has an angled face that many say resembles an aircraft's wing.

➕ E10 ✉ 200 Park Avenue
✋ Free 🍴 Various restaurants ($$) and cafés ($) on plaza level
🚇 42nd Street

MUSEUM OF ARTS AND DESIGN

Formerly the American Craft Museum, this collection features pottery, textiles, furnishings, and sculpture. Compiled from loaned pieces and selections from the permanent holdings, exhibitions usually last several months.

www.americancraftmuseum.org

✚ D9 ✉ 40 W 53rd Street ☎ 212/956-3535 ⏰ Daily 10–6, Thu until 8 ✋ Moderate 🚇 Fifth Avenue

MUSEUM OF MODERN ART

Best places to see, ➤ 50–51.

NEW YORK PUBLIC LIBRARY

The city's pre-eminent reference library and an architectural masterpiece, New York Public Library is guarded by a celebrated pair of stone lions, named Fortitude and

Patience by Mayor Fiorello La Guardia in the 1930s. Inside, the splendors of the *beaux arts* design—such as the DeWitt Wallace Periodical Room and the wonderful mural lining the McGraw Rotunda on the third floor—are best discovered with the free guided tours. Various changing exhibitions in the side rooms, usually on themes of art and history, provide a further excuse to wander the magnificent corridors.

www.nypl.org

🚩 D11 ✉ Fifth Avenue at 42nd Street ☎ 212/930-0830 🕐 Tue and Wed 11–7:30, Mon, Thu–Sat 11–6, Sun 1–5 ✋ Free 🚇 42nd Street ❓ Free guided tours Mon–Sat at 11 and 2, Sun at 2

PALEY CENTER FOR MEDIA

The museum is actually an archive of U.S. television and radio, made available from a computerized cataloguing system. Selections from the 75,000 programs and commercials can be watched or listened to in private consoles, but most visitors will be content with the varied televisual selections screened each day.

www.mtr.org

🚩 D9 ✉ 25 W 52nd Street ☎ 212/621-6800 🕐 Tue–Sun noon–6 (Thu also 6–8) ✋ Moderate 🍴 Café ($$) 🚇 Fifth Avenue–53rd Street

ROCKEFELLER CENTER

Rockefeller Center arose through the 1930s to become a widely admired complex of streamlined limestone and aluminum buildings that form an aesthetically satisfying whole, despite being designed by different architects.

Intended to provide a welcoming environment where people could work, shop, eat, and be entertained, structures such as Radio City Music Hall and the RCA Building (now the GE Building) became noted city landmarks. The labyrinthine walkways are filled with eye-catching art deco decoration while the Plaza provides a setting for outdoor dining during the summer and becomes a much-loved skating rink during the winter. Top of the Rock is an observation deck on the 67th–70th floor, open (for a fee) 8:30am–midnight all year.

www.rockefellercenter.com

🛉 D10 ✉ Bordered by Fifth and Seventh avenues, 47th and 52nd streets ☎ Tours 212/664-3700
🕐 Always open 🎫 Free 🍴 Various restaurants and cafés ($–$$$)
Ⓜ Rockefeller Center ❓ Tours (moderate/expensive)

ROOSEVELT ISLAND

Roosevelt Island is a long, thin strip of land between Manhattan and Queens and a curious piece of New York that few visitors ever become aware of. Take the short cable-car ride, the Roosevelt Island Tramway. The island once held hospitals providing for the terminally sick and mentally ill.

The ruins of the old hospitals (enhanced by avant-garde sculpture) stand on the island's southern end, while much of the rest has been developed since the 1970s as a car-free housing development by architects Philip Johnson and John Burgee. The 147-acre (60ha) island has five parks and interesting views of Manhattan and makes for an intriguing detour, if only to see Manhattan from a different angle.

✚ F8 (off map) ✉ East River, between Manhattan and Queens
🚇 Roosevelt Island; also cable car from terminal 60th Street and Second Avenue

ST. PATRICK'S CATHEDRAL

Nowhere else in Midtown Manhattan is there a sense of peace and tranquility matching that found inside St. Patrick's Cathedral, at its best when its interior is illuminated by candlelight. In a loosely interpreted French Gothic style, the cathedral was completed in 1878 by celebrated architect James Renwick; the twin towers that rise to 330ft (100m) were unveiled 10 years later. Despite being enclosed by modern high rises, the Roman Catholic cathedral, the largest in the U.S., retains its sense of majesty.

www.saintpatrickscathedral.org

➕ D10 ✉ Fifth Avenue, 50th and 51st streets 🕐 6:30am–8:45pm ✋ Free
🚇 Fifth Avenue–53rd Street

SEAGRAM BUILDING

Ground-breaking architecture is prevalent in Manhattan, but no single building is perhaps more influential than Mies Van Der Rohe's Seagram Building, completed in 1958 and widely regarded as the perfect expression of the International Style. Rising 38 stories in glass and bronze, the Seagram Building also gave New York its first plaza, a feature that subsequently became common with high-rise development, sometimes being enclosed to form atriums. Walk into the lobby to peek into the Philip Johnson-designed Four Seasons restaurant.

✚ E9 ✉ 375 Park Avenue ⌚ Lobby: Mon–Fri 9–5 ✋ Free 🍴 Four Seasons restaurant ($$$) 🚇 51st Street–Lexington Avenue ❓ Tours Tue at 3 ☎ 212/572-7000

TIMES SQUARE

Best places to see,
➤ 54–55.

TRUMP TOWER

The New York of the 1980s was the domain of the yuppie, and perhaps no greater role model existed for the rapid creation of wealth than high-profile property developer Donald Trump. A heady mix of vulgarity, ingenuity, and flamboyance, Trump Tower is a symbol both of the man and the decade's economic boom. The upper levels hold luxury apartments while the lower floors include the famous pink stone atrium and a gathering of luxury retail outlets and restaurants. The interior atrium includes a seven-story waterfall.

✚ D9 ✉ 725 Fifth Avenue
☎ 212/832-2000 🕐 Daily 8am–10pm ✋ Free
🍴 Numerous restaurants and cafés ($–$$$) 🚇 Fifth Avenue–53rd Street

UNITED NATIONS HEADQUARTERS

The United Nations has been based in New York since 1947, much of its administrative activity being carried out in the unmistakable Le Corbusier-designed Secretariat Building rising above the East River. Public admission is by guided tour, which provides an informative hour-long sweep through the U.N.'s interior, including the General Assembly building and the Security Council Chambers. Outside, the 18-acre (7ha) grounds hold parks, gardens, and abundant monuments.

www.un.org/tours

✚ F10 ✉ First Avenue at 46th Street
☎ 212/963-8687 ⏱ Guided tours daily
9:30–4:45. Closed weekends in Jan and
Feb ✋ Expensive 🍴 Restaurant ($$$),
café ($) 🚇 42nd Street–Grand Central

HOTELS

Belvedere Hotel ($$)

Part of the Empire Hotel group, the Belvedere offers large, well-furnished rooms with kitchenettes equipped with a microwave, refrigerator, and coffeemaker. If you don't want to do your own cooking, try the hotel's Brazilian steakhouse.

✉ 319 W 48th Street ☎ 212/245-7000; www.belvederehotelnyc.com

🚇 50th Street

♦♦ Best Western President Hotel ($$)

Part of a large hotel group with several Manhattan locations, this facility is in the heart of Broadway. Rooms are comfortable and have all the expected amenities.

✉ 234 48th Street ☎ 212/246-8800; www.bestwesternnewyork.com

🚇 49th Street

♦♦ Edison ($–$$)

See page 78.

♦♦♦♦ Four Seasons ($$$)

See page 78.

♦♦♦ Hilton Times Square ($$–$$$)

The Hilton is in the heart of the Times Square district and has quiet if bland rooms, all above the 21st floor, with wonderful views.

✉ 234 W 42nd Street ☎ 212/840-8222; www.hilton.com

🚇 Times Square–42nd Street

♦♦♦♦ Le Parker Meridien ($$$)

See page 78.

♦♦♦♦ Michelangelo ($$$)

The 18th- and 19th-century European art, marble and crystal, and spacious rooms help the Michelangelo rank among New York's most luxurious hotels.

✉ 152 W 51st Street ☎ 212/765-0505; www.michelangelohotel.com

🚇 7th Avenue or Rockefeller Center

▼▼ ▼▼ The Muse ($$$)

A boutique hotel decorated in warm woods and soft pastels, with friendly service and deluxe apartments.

✉ 130 W 46th Street ☎ 212/485-2400; www.themusehotel.com
🚇 42nd Street

Roger Smith ($$)

Tastefully furnished rooms, great service and sensible rates are the appeal of this small hotel in Midtown. Enjoy a meal or a drink in Lily's bar/restaurant, with its murals and sculpture.

✉ 501 Lexington Avenue ☎ 212/755-1400; www.rogersmith.com
🚇 51st Street–Lexington Avenue

▼▼▼ Royalton ($$)

In Midtown and close to shopping at Fifth Avenue, the interiors are designed by Philippe Starck, and the ultra-modern white lobby is a chic place for a drink; the Round Bar is a cozy alternative. The rooms are decorated in contemporary minimalist style.

✉ 44 W 44th Street ☎ 212/869-4400; www.royaltonhotel.com
🚇 42nd Street

RESTAURANTS

▼▼▼ "21" Club ($$$)

Despite the hamburger on the menu, this is sophisticated dining in stylish surroundings. Rub shoulders with celebrities in the Bar Room, and sample a bottle from the Prohibition-era wine cellar.

✉ 21 W 52nd Street between Fifth and Sixth avenues ☎ 212/582-7200; www.21club.com 🕐 Mon–Fri 12–2:30, Mon–Thu 5:30–10 Fri–Sat 5:30–11; closed Sun 🚇 47th–50th streets

▼▼▼ Blue Fin ($$$)

Enjoy the freshest fish at this multilevel restaurant and bar, part of a restaurant group specializing in seafood. You can try sushi on the upper floor and choose from more than 600 wines.

✉ W Hotel Times Square, 1567 Broadway ☎ 212/918-1400; www.brguestrestaurants.com 🕐 Breakfast, lunch and dinner 🚇 49th Street

Brooklyn Diner USA ($–$$)

Brash and enjoyable pseudo-traditional diner, with big breakfasts and bigger sandwiches, alongside burgers, assorted milkshakes, and the chance to round off the meal with a hot fudge sundae.

✉ 212 W 57th Street ☎ 212/977-1957; www.brooklyndiner.com

🅖 Breakfast, lunch and dinner ④ 57th Street–Seventh Street

▼Carnegie Deli ($–$$)

Huge portions of classic Jewish fare such as matzo balls, knishes, pastrami and cheesecake. Open until 4am.

✉ 854 Seventh Avenue ☎ 212/757-2245; www.carnegiedeli.com

🅖 Breakfast, lunch and dinner 🚇 57th Street

▼▼Chevys Fresh Mex ($$)

Part of a nationwide chain but a handy location to sample a big range of fajitas, tortillas and other Mexican fare.

✉ 259 W 42nd Street ☎ 212/302-4010 🅖 Lunch and dinner

🚇 Times Square–42nd Street

▼▼Diwan ($$)

This Indian restaurant serves a wide range of flavorful fare. Try the tasting menu to experience an unending procession of dishes, each one as delicious as the next.

✉ 148 E 48th Street between Lexington and Third avenues ☎ 212/593-5425; www.diwanrestaurant.com 🅖 Mon–Thu 11:30–2:30, 5–10:30, Fri 11:30–2:30, 5–11, Sat–Sun 5–11 🚇 51st Street (6)

Edison Cafe ($–$$)

Off the lobby of the art deco Edison Hotel, this busy diner has a full range of diner staples for breakfast, lunch and dinner, with a few Jewish and Polish specialties also on the menu.

✉ 228 W 47th Street ☎ 212/840-5000 🅖 Breakfast, lunch and dinner

🚇 50th Street

Ellen's Stardust Diner ($–$$)

Retro-diner packed with "1950s" memorablia and staff regularly bursting into song; the menu offers classic diner fare such as meatloaf, waffles, burgers and milkshakes, but the theatrical staff and setting are the draw.

✉ 1650 Broadway ☎ 212/956-5151; www.ellensstardustdiner.com
🕐 Breakfast, lunch and dinner 🚇 50th Street

▼▼▼ Four Seasons ($$$)
See page 60.

Gordon Ramsay at The London ($$–$$$)
Just a year after opening his New York venture in 2006, Britain's celebrity chef won two Michelin stars for his impeccable, beautifully presented cuisine. Book at least two months ahead as tables are snapped up instantly. Even those on a budget can treat themselves to the 3-course, prix fixe lunch at $45.

✉ 151 West 54th Street between 6th and 7th avenues ☎ 212/468-8888; www.gordonramsay.com 🕐 Lunch and dinner 🚇 Seventh Avenue

▼▼ John's Pizzeria ($$)
See page 61.

▼▼ Mars 2112 ($$)
Among the most imaginative of the city's many theme restaurants. Diners mingle with extra-terrestrials while sampling "inter galactic fusion cuisine" that bears a surprising similarity to fashionable American diner fare.

✉ Corner of 51st and Broadway ☎ 212/582-2112; www.mars2112.com
🕐 Lunch and dinner 🚇 50th Street

▼▼▼ Molyvos ($$)
The lunch menu features everything from grilled baby octopus to a filling eggplant (aubergine) moussaka; while even heartier dinner fare includes traditional favorites such as marinated lamb shanks and whole grilled fish. Don't miss the delicious Greek dips, and the good range of Greek and Mediterranean wines.

✉ 871 Seventh Avenue between W 55th and 56th streets ☎ 212/582-7500; www.molyvos.com 🕐 Mon–Sat 12–3, 5:30–11:30, Sun 12–11
🚇 Seventh Avenue

♦♦ ♦♦ Oceana ($$$)

The French-Asian cuisine here created by chef Cornelius Gallagher is bold and often surprising, producing delights such as the Loup de Mer en Croûte with bok choy, tamarind and wasabi. There is an enormous international wine cellar, and a wine-tasting menu is also available.

✉ 55 E 54th Street between Madison and Park avenues ☎ 212/759-5941; www.oceanarestaurant.com ◉ Mon–Fri 12–2:30, Mon–Fri 5:30–10:30, Sat 5–10:30 🚇 53rd Street/Fifth Avenue (E, V)

♦♦ ♦♦ The Sea Grill ($$$)

Cool blue decor creates a suitably ocean-like setting in Rockefeller Center for the creations of one of the city's finest seafood chefs; choose from Chilean sea bass, crab cakes, mahi-mahi and lots more, inventively cooked and stylishly presented.

✉ 19 W 49th Street ☎ 212/332-7610; www.theseagrillnyc.com ◉ Lunch and dinner; closed Sun, dinner only Sat 🚇 49th Street

♦♦ Victor's Café ($$–$$$)

See page 59.

♦♦ ♦ Virgil's Real Barbecue ($$)

Southern-style barbecue menu is the theme at this large restaurant. Choices include BBQ chicken with mashed potatoes or vast plates of Memphis-style barbecue.

✉ 152 W 44th Street ☎ 212/921-9494; www.virgilsbbq.com ◉ Lunch and dinner 🚇 42nd Street–Times Square

♦♦ ♦ Vong ($$)

After living in eastern Asia in the 1980s, French chef Jean-Georges was revolutionary in bringing together French and Asian cuisine. Flavors of lemongrass, cilantro, ginger and coconut milk continue to influence the dishes here, creating delicious and inventive French-Asian combinations that dance on the tongue.

✉ 200 E 54th Street at Third Avenue ☎ 212/486-9592
◉ Mon–Fri 12–2:30, 6–11, Sat 5–11, Sun 5:30–9
🚇 53rd Street/Lexington Avenue

44 & X Hell's Kitchen ($$–$$$)

Traditional American fare given a fine-dining treatment: meatloaf, waffles, salmon, steaks and ribs all get a classy makeover.

✉ 622 10th Avenue ☎ 212/977-1170; www.44andX.com 🕐 Dinner; brunch on weekends 🚇 42nd Street

SHOPPING

DEPARTMENT STORES

Sak's Fifth Avenue
See page 81.

Takashimaya
See page 81.

CLOTHES AND ACCESSORIES

Brooks Brothers
From overcoats to suits and shirts, conservative men's clothing rarely comes in a better quality than that found here.

✉ 346 Madison Avenue ☎ 212/682-8800; www.brooksbrothers.com 🚇 Grand Central

Cartier
Gold, silverware and porcelain that is the stuff of dreams; prices reach the realms of the phantasmagorical.

✉ 653 Fifth Avenue ☎ 212/753-0111 🚇 53rd Street–Fifth Avenue

The Shirt Store
Discerning shirt wearers can choose from among eight collars and many types of cotton and have their chosen design made to order.

✉ 51 E 44th Street ☎ 212/557-8040; www.shirtstore.com 🚇 Grand Central

BOOKS, CDS AND RECORDS

Colony Music
Mainstream and obscure recordings from stage shows and other musical genres, plus sheet music, posters, concert programs and assorted memorabilia.

✉ 1619 Broadway ☎ 212/265-2050; www.colonymusic.com 🚇 50th Street

Rizzoli Bookstore

A cozy general bookstore with particularly good stocks of art and photography titles, including discount bargains.

✉ W 57th Street ☎ 212/759-2424; www.rizzoliusa.com 🚇 57th Street

SPORTS EQUIPMENT
World of Golf

The name says it all: Packed with golf clubs, bags, balls, shirts, caps, books, videos, CDs and even more things connected with golf.

✉ 147 E 47th Street ☎ 212/755-9398; www.twog.com 🚇 51st Street; Lexington–Third Avenue

ENTERTAINMENT

LIVE MUSIC
BB King Blues Club and Grill

Part of the new-look Times Square, this fashionable supper club focuses on blues, but also features rock, jazz and other genres.

✉ 237 W 42nd Street ☎ 212/997-4144; www.bbkingblues.com 🚇 42nd Street–Times Square

Iridium

Appealing medium-sized venue showcasing accomplished jazz names and talents on the rise.

✉ 1650 Broadway ☎ 212/582-2121; www.iridiumjazzclub.com 🚇 49th Street

CINEMA
Ziegfeld

A sumptuous place to see a movie. Sink into one of the 1,131 velvet seats and relax.

✉ 141 West 54th Street ☎ 212/777-3456 or 212/307-1862 🚇 57th Street–Seventh Avenue

BAR
Top of the Tower

See page 77.

Uptown and Central Park

During the 19th century many of New York's wealthy moved north and settled on either side of the newly created Central Park, in what became the Upper East Side and the Upper West Side.

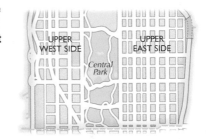

The Upper East Side became fashionable in the 1890s when the top families in New York society began erecting mock-European mansions along Fifth Avenue, facing Central Park. Comfortable brownstone townhouses sprouted on adjoining streets, now also dotted with smart apartment buildings.

The main shopping street of the Upper East Side is Madison Avenue, which provides locals with antique shops, art galleries, boutiques, restaurants, and dog-grooming specialists.

The Dakota Building (➤ 112) set the tone for the Upper West Side and many more luxury apartment buildings through the late 1800s as residential development quickly filled the area between Central Park and the Hudson River. After years of decline in the mid-20th century, writers and professors and professionals with young families discovered the spacious "pre-war" apartments with views of the Hudson River, and the neighborhood became a liberal enclave to the East Side's blue-blooded conservatism.

Away from the quiet side streets, the commercial arteries hold a mix of furniture retailers, gourmet delis and fashionable ethnic eateries. Zabar's gourmet food store on Broadway is at the heart of the West Side's shopping area.

AMERICAN MUSEUM OF NATURAL HISTORY

The American Museum of Natural History was founded in 1861 and, with roughly 36 million exhibits drawn from every corner of the globe, is now the world's largest museum.

The fossil and dinosaur halls are places to admire five-story-high dinosaur skeletons and to experience state-of-the-art exhibits exploring the origins of life on earth from the Jurassic period onwards. A 94ft (28m) model blue whale, the world's largest mammal, hangs above the other exhibits in the Hall of Ocean Life. A butterfly conservatory is open October to June. Dioramas portray bird and animal life and displays about humankind include halls devoted to Native Americans and the peoples of Africa, Asia, and South and Central America.

Alongside the museum, a steel and glass cube provides a striking transparent exterior for the Rose Center for Earth and Space. Inside is the Hayden Planetarium, where the show The Search For Life: Are We Alone, is narrated by actor Harrison Ford. A series of walkways and galleries hold displays on astronomical subjects and an IMAX theater shows films on natural topics.

www.amnh.org

🚼 C5 ✉ Central Park West at 79th Street ☎ 212/769-5100 🕒 Daily 10–5:45 🖐 Expensive 🍴 Cafeteria ($) and cafés ($$) 🚇 81st Street

ASIA SOCIETY

Founded by John D. Rockefeller III in 1956, the Asia Society holds an impressive collection of Asian art, including wonderful Edo-period Japanese prints, pre-Angkor Cambodian sculpture and 11th-century Chinese ceramics.

The broader purpose of the society, which has centers around the U.S. and the Pacific rim, is to promote greater understanding between Asia and the U.S. To this end, it hosts an ongoing series of movies, concerts, lectures, and workshops on Asian themes.

www.asiasociety.org

✠ E7 ✉ 725 Park Avenue ☎ 212/288-6400 ⏰ Tue–Sun 11–6, Fri until 9 ✋ Moderate 🍴 Café ($$) 🚇 68th Street–Hunter College

CATHEDRAL CHURCH OF ST. JOHN THE DIVINE

The seat of the Episcopal Diocese of New York, the largest Gothic-style cathedral in the world (it covers 11 acres/4.5ha), is still unfinished. The cornerstone was laid in 1892 but wars, the death of the architect, changes in design, and shortages of money have resulted in sporadic building work. The cathedral is now two-thirds complete, and no new construction is planned for the immediate future. Exhibitions fill the various nooks and crannies.

www.stjohndivine.org

🔲 B1 ✉ 1047 Amsterdam Avenue ☎ 212/316-7540 🕐 Daily 7:30–6
✋ Tours moderate Ⓜ Cathedral Parkway ❓ Tours Tue–Sat 11, Sun 1

CENTRAL PARK

Best places to see, ➤ 36–37.

THE CLOISTERS

Medieval European monastic buildings might be the last thing anyone would expect to find in Manhattan, but the Cloisters are exactly that. Assembled on a site overlooking the Hudson River, these bits and pieces of five French monasteries collected in the early 1900s now showcase the
Metropolitan Museum of Art's medieval holdings. The contents are a feast of 12th- to 15th-century creativity, but the show-stealer is the setting, with its splendid views.

www.metmuseum.org

🔲 A1 (off map) ✉ Fort Tryon Park, Washington Heights ☎ 212/923-3700
🕐 Mar–Oct Tue–Sun 9:30–5:15; Nov–Feb Tue–Sun 9:30–4:45 ✋ Expensive
🍴 Café ($) Ⓜ 190th Street

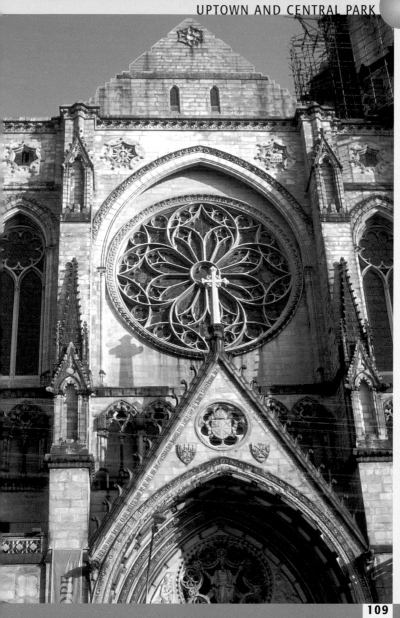

COLUMBIA UNIVERSITY

Founded by royal charter of British king George II
in 1754, King's College, Columbia is the oldest
institution of higher learning in the U.S. It has steadily
moved northwards up Manhattan, arriving at its
present site in 1897. The predominantly red-brick
campus buildings, reflecting turn-of-the-20th-century
American collegiate architecture, are grouped around
compact plazas on 32 acres (13ha). Inside the Low
Library (based on Rome's Pantheon), at the heart of
the complex, are displays tracing the history of the
university.

www.columbia.edu

✚ A1 (off map) ✉ 116th and Broadway ☎ 212/854-4900
🕐 Visit during daylight hours ✋ Free Ⓜ 116th Street
❓ Tours 1pm weekdays
ℹ Visitor Center at 213 Low Memorial Library

COOPER-HEWITT NATIONAL DESIGN
MUSEUM

Part of the Smithsonian Institution, the museum,
housed in the former mansion of steel mogul Andrew
Carnegie, explores design and decorative arts from

wall coverings and textiles to graphic arts and product design. The collection began with the oddments the three Hewitt sisters picked up on a visit to London in 1897. The fenced garden offers a tranquil oasis along Fifth Avenue.

http://cooperhewitt.org

✚ D4 ✉ 2 E 91st Street ☎ 212/849-8400 🕙 Mon–Thu 10–5, Fri 10–9, Sat 10–6, Sun noon–6 💲 Expensive 🍴 Café ($) 🚇 86th Street

DAKOTA BUILDING

Destined to be remembered by the world as the place where ex-Beatle John Lennon was fatally shot in 1980, the Dakota Building had already earned a place in the annals of New York history by being one of the city's first specially designed luxury apartment buildings. Erected in the 1880s, the Dakota steadily attracted the rich and famous to reside within its German Gothic/French Renaissance façade, and remains a prestigious address.

✚ C6 ✉ 72nd Street and Central Park West ⊗ Private residence; view from street only ⊗ 72nd Street

EAST HARLEM

Once known as "Italian Harlem," East Harlem has been the main base of New York's Puerto Rican population, known locally as "El Barrio," since the 1930s and 1940s. Although predominantly Puerto Rican, Mexicans and other Latin Americans also figure among the Spanish-speaking population, and the area is growing more diverse as real estate prices on the Upper East Side continue to rise. The center of activity is 115th Street and Park Avenue, where some 30 stalls of La Marqueta (the Market) proffer sugar cane, yams, and papaya, and other culinary delights of the island, while sounds of salsa reverberate in the air.

✚ E1 ✉ First Avenue to Fifth Avenue, E 96th Street to E 125th Street 🚇 110th Street or 116th Street

EL MUSEO DEL BARRIO

With strong links to the local East Harlem community, El Museo del Barrio grew from a local school classroom into a museum devoted to the cultures of Latin America, particularly Puerto Rico. There is a small permanent collection of pre-Columbian objects, but greater prominence is accorded to many temporary exhibitions documenting facets of Latin American history and culture.

www.elmuseo.org

✚ D2 ✉ 1230 Fifth Avenue ☎ 212/831-7272 🕐 Wed–Sun 11–5 ✋ Moderate 🚇 103rd Street

FRICK COLLECTION

Henry Clay Frick made his money in the late 19th century, and filled his mansion on Fifth Avenue with an outstanding art collection. The relative intimacy of the setting is as enjoyable as the paintings, sculptures and decorative items. El Greco, Titian, Rembrandt and Turner are just a few of the painters represented by exceptional canvases, while two rococo delights—Fragonard's *Progress of Love* series and Boucher's *Arts and Science* series— each occupy a room of their own. Other highlights include Gainsborough's *The Mall in St James's Park* and Rembrandt's 1658 *Self-Portrait*.

www.frick.org

➕ D7 ✉ 1 E 70th Street ☎ 212/288-0700 🕐 Tue–Sun 10–6 ✋ Expensive
🚇 68th Street–Hunter College

GRACIE MANSION

Standing deep in today's modern metropolis, it is difficult to imagine that, on its completion in 1799, Gracie Mansion served its owner, Scottish merchant Archibald Gracie, as a country retreat and that the 16-room house became familiar to many of the city's influential figures. But the War of 1812 decimated Gracie's trade and the house was sold in 1823. The Museum of the City of New York was among the subsequent occupants until 1942, when the house became the official residence of New York's mayor. It now houses a huge collection of American-made furniture and fixtures.

www.nyc.gov

➕ F4 (off map) ✉ East End Avenue at 88th Street ☎ 212/639-9675
🕐 Guided tours only Wed 10–3 (pre-reserved) ✋ Moderate 🚇 86th Street

GRANT'S TOMB

Rising from obscurity to mastermind the battlefield strategies that helped the Union side triumph in the Civil War, General Ulysses S. Grant became one of the best-known Americans of his time and was president from 1869 to 1877. A million people lined the route of the parade and dedication ceremony in 1897 of what is the largest mausoleum in North America, and a resting place commensurate with his status. In addition to the 9-ton granite sarcophagi of Grant and his wife, exhibits depict Grant's life and accomplishments.

www.nps.gov/gegr

✚ A1 (off map) ✉ Riverside Drive at 122nd Street ☎ 212/666-1640
🕐 Daily 9–5 ✋ Free 🚇 125th Street

GUGGENHEIM MUSEUM

Best places to see, ➤ 46–47.

HARLEM

Many of the tens of thousands of African–Americans who arrived in New York in the early 1900s settled in brownstone townhouses in what had been a German–Jewish neighborhood. By the 1920s the neighborhood had become the U.S.'s most culturally vibrant black urban area.

Partly dilapidated, partly gentrified, Harlem holds landmarks such as the Apollo Theater (253 125th Street) and Abyssinian Baptist Church (132 Odell Clark Place), one of hundreds of churches where gospel singing draws tourists along with neighborhood faithful.

✚ C1 (off map) ✉ North of Cathedral Parkway; west of Fifth Avenue 🚇 125th Street

JEWISH MUSEUM

An imitation French Gothic château erected in 1909 for banker Felix M. Warburg provides an impressive home for the largest collection of Jewish ceremonial art and historical objects in the U.S. Among the enormous collection are household objects, coins and religious pieces dating back to the Roman era that help create a picture of Jewish life from early times to the modern day. Special exhibits focus on Jewish history and art.

www.jewishmuseum.org

✚ D4 ✉ 1109 Fifth Avenue ☎ 212/423-3200
🕐 Sat–Wed 11–5:45, Thu 11–8. Closed public and Jewish holidays ✋ Expensive 🍴 Kosher café ($)
🚇 92nd Street

LINCOLN CENTER FOR THE PERFORMING ARTS

Part of what was once known as Hell's Kitchen and the setting for the musical *West Side Story* is now the multi-building complex of Lincoln Center for the Performing Arts. Since its 1960s completion, the center has provided homes for a dozen resident cultural organizations, including the New York Philharmonic, the Metropolitan Opera, the New York State Theater, and the Juilliard School for the Performing Arts, all grouped on or close to a central plaza.

www.lincolncenter.org

✛ B8 ✉ Broadway at 64th Street ☎ 212/546-2656; 212/875 5350 (tours) ✋ Free to visit; charges for performances 🍴 Various restaurants and cafés ($–$$$) 🚇 66th Street–Lincoln Center ❓ Daily tours; outdoor concerts in summer

METROPOLITAN MUSEUM OF ART

Best places to see, ➤ 48–49.

MUSEUM OF THE CITY OF NEW YORK

This museum tells of the city's evolution from Colonial settlement to international metropolis with photographs, costumes, maps, and other objects from its collection. Among the permanent exhibits are a history of theater in New York and a collection of toys used by generations of New York children.

www.mcny.org

✚ D2 ✉ 1220 Fifth Avenue ☎ 212/534-1672 ⏰ Tue–Sun 10–5
✋ Donation, moderate Ⓜ 103rd Street

NEW-YORK HISTORICAL SOCIETY

The hyphen in its name dates from the society's founding in 1804, a time when the city was spelled that way and when no other museum existed to receive the many bequests of wealthy New Yorkers. Consequently the society acquired a tremendous batch of art, from amateurish though historically important portraits of rich city dwellers to seminal works by the Hudson River School painters and fine furniture from the Federal period. Highlights here include a substantial collection of Tiffany glasswork and the watercolors of John James Audubon's *Birds of America* series.

www.nyhistory.org

➕ C6 ✉ 2 W 77th Street ☎ 212/873-3400 🕐 Tue–Sat 10–6 (Fri until 8), Sun 11–5:45 ✋ Moderate 🚇 81st Street

RIVERSIDE CHURCH

Largely financed by John D. Rockefeller Jr., the French Gothic Riverside Church has loomed high alongside the Hudson River since 1930. Intended to serve its membership's recreational as well as religious needs, the church has at times held schoolrooms, a gym, a theater and even a bowling alley. Originally Baptist but now interdenominational, the church's tower, 392ft (120m) high, houses the world's largest carillon.

www.theriversidechurch.org

➕ A1 (off map) ✉ 490 Riverside Drive ☎ 212/870-6700 🕒 Tue–Sun 9–5 ✋ Free 🚇 116th Street ❓ Sun carillon concerts; guided tours after Sun service

WHITNEY MUSEUM OF AMERICAN ART

When the Metropolitan Museum of Art rejected her collection of American painting and sculpture, Gertrude Vanderbilt Whitney responded by creating her own museum in 1931, and with it continued her long devotion to supporting new American art. The collection is now housed in Marcel Breurer's "brutalist" inverted ziggurat of concrete and granite.

Often controversial and devoting much of its space to relatively unknown work, the Whitney has an incredible collection of works by major U.S. names such as Rothko, Johns, and Warhol who are represented in the permanent collection. Three galleries are devoted to Calder, O'Keeffe, and Hopper.

www.whitney.org

➕ E6 ✉ 945 Madison Avenue ☎ 212/570-3676 🕒 Wed–Thu and Sat–Sun 11–6, Fri 1–9 ✋ Expensive 🍴 Café ($) 🚇 77th Street ❓ Lectures, films

HOTELS

♦♦♦ Affinia Gardens Hotel ($$$)
See page 78.

♦♦♦♦ Carlyle ($$$)
See page 78.

♦♦♦ Excelsior Hotel ($$)
Recently renovated in a French motif, this hotel, across from the Museum of Natural History, has comfortable rooms and a lounge on the second floor with a working fireplace.
✉ 45 W 81st Street ☎ 212/362-9200; www.excelsiorhotelny.org
🚇 81st Street

♦♦ Franklin ($$)
See page 78.

Hotel Belleclaire ($$)
This art deco hotel in a landmark building was renovated in 2004. It offers large, stylish rooms at good prices for New York City.
✉ 250 W 77th Street ☎ 212/362-7700; www.hotelbelleclaire.com
🚇 79th Street

♦♦♦♦ Hotel Plaza Athénée ($$$)
The luxury begins at the plush lobby and continues through to the ultra-comfortable rooms with European-style furnishings and with rose marble bathrooms. Rooms above the 12th floor boast cinematic views. The restaurant is French, the bar Moroccan-themed.
✉ 37 E 64th Street ☎ 212/734-9100; www.plaza-athenee.com
🚇 68th Street–Hunter College

♦♦♦ The Lucerne ($$–$$$)
See page 79.

♦♦♦♦♦ Ritz-Carlton New York, Central Park ($$$)
See page 79.

RESTAURANTS

Brother Jimmy's ($)

"The Bait Shack" branch of a restaurant with a few Manhattan locations, this sometimes rowdy spot offers substantial sandwiches, soups, barbecued ribs, and other accompaniments to beer drinking and watching sports TV.

✉ 1644 Third Avenue ☎ 212/426-2020; www.brotherjimmys.com ⊙ Lunch and dinner ⓡ 96th Street

♥♥♥ Café Boulud ($$$)

Another restaurant from Daniel Boulud, this sophisticated eatery is inspired by 1930s Paris, but you'll find dishes from as far afield as Vietnam, Morocco, and the Caribbean.

✉ 20 E 76th Street ☎ 212/772-2600; www.danielnyc.com ⊙ Lunch and dinner; Sun–Mon dinner only ⓡ 77th Street

♥♥♥ Café Luxembourg ($$$)

Lastingly popular French-style brasserie near Lincoln Center that draws knowledgeable diners to its eclectic, seasonal menu.

✉ 200 W 70th Street ☎ 212/873-7411 ⊙ Lunch and dinner
ⓡ 72nd Street

♥♥ Carmine's ($–$$)

Bring your appetite and lots of friends. The tasty southern Italian dishes are served in abundant portions that are meant to be shared, with all the friendly, family-style bustle that characterizes old New York.

✉ 2450 Broadway ☎ 212/362-2200 ⊙ Lunch and dinner ⓡ 86th Street

Ciao Bella Gelato Cafe ($)

A hole-in-the-wall provider of sorbets, frozen yogurt and ice cream in myriad flavors, certain to cool and calm the most demanding customer.

✉ 27 E 92nd Street ☎ 212/831-5555 ⊙ All day ⓡ 96th Street

♥♥♥ Daniel ($$$)

See page 60.

Elaine's ($$–$$$)

The scene's the thing more than the food at this favorite hangout of Upper East Side celebs.

✉ 1703 Second Avenue ☎ 212/534-8103 🍴 Dinner 🚇 86th Street

Ollie's Noodle Shop ($$–$$$)

Fresh and authentic Chinese fare at very reasonable prices.

✉ 1991 Broadway ☎ 212/595-8181 🍴 Lunch and dinner
🚇 Lincoln Center

Popover Café ($–$$)

Pastry "popovers" and a range of soups, sandwiches and salads make this one of the neighborhood's most popular stops.

✉ 551 Amsterdam Avenue ☎ 212/595-8555 🍴 Breakfast, lunch and dinner
🚇 86th Street

SHOPPING

DEPARTMENT STORES

Barney's New York

See page 80.

Bergdorf Goodman

See page 80.

Bloomingdale's

A sophisticated shopper's haven since 1886 and once the epitome of a certain Upper East Side milieu, this huge art deco landmark department store carries stylish, midpriced clothing, accessories, and housewares.

✉ 1000 Third Avenue ☎ 212/705-2000 🚇 59th Street

ART AND ANTIQUITIES

A La Vieille Russie

Quality antique jewelry, many of them representing the handiwork of the finest craftsmen of Tsarist Russia.

✉ 781 Fifth Avenue ☎ 212/752-1727; www.alvr.com 🚇 Lexington Avenue–59th Street

Leo Castelli Gallery

A gallery renowned for bringing the work of abstract expressionist and pop art notables to a wider audience, and still offering their works to well-heeled collectors.

✉ 18 E 77th Street ☎ 212/249-4470; www.castelligallery.com
🚇 77th Street

Manhattan Art and Antiques Center

More than 100 galleries under one roof to provide hours of browsing delight for the committed art and antique seeker.

✉ 1050 Second Avenue ☎ 212/355-4400; www.the-maac.com
🚇 59th Street

Pace Wildenstein

Prestigious gallery for the heavyweights of modern and contemporary art; particularly noted for rising names. Also with galleries in Chelsea.

✉ 32 E 57th Street ☎ 212/421-3292; www.pacewildenstein.com
🚇 Lexington Avenue–59th Street

CLOTHES AND ACCESSORIES

Betsey Johnson

Bold and colorful female fashions that fall just short of daring. Also at several other city locations.

✉ 251 E 60th Street ☎ 212/319-7699; www.betsyjohnson.com
🚇 Lexington Avenue–59th Street

David Webb

If five-figure price tags do not deter, this is the place to select that special diamond, emerald, sapphire, or pearl, fashioned into rings, brooches, cufflinks or encrusted onto boxes.

✉ 789 Madison Aveunue ☎ 212/421-3030; www.davidwebb.com
🚇 68th Street

Encore

Well positioned to catch the barely worn cast-offs of Upper East Side high society, this consignment store is a top spot for rummaging through racks of designerwear at almost affordable prices.

✉ 1132 Madison Avenue ☎ 212/879-2850; www.encoresale.com
🚇 86th Street

Hermès

Top-dollar silk scarves, perfume, handbags, belts and beautiful baby gifts.

✉ 691 Madison Avenue ☎ 212/751-3181; www.hermes.com
🚇 59th Street–Lexington Avenue

Polo/Ralph Lauren

The designer has a cluster of shops on Madison and in malls everywhere. This store sports top-notch tweeds, cotton shirts, and everything else.

✉ 867 Madison Avenue ☎ 212/606-2100; www.polo.com
🚇 68th Street–Hunter College

Tiffany & Co

Flagship store of Tiffany & Co, founded in 1837, with three floors of crystal, gold and silverware, clocks, and jewelry. The opening scene of *Breakfast at Tiffany's* (1961) was filmed here.

✉ 727 Fifth Avenue ☎ 212/755-8000; www.tiffany.com
🚇 59th Street

GIFTS, ODDITIES AND COLLECTIBLES
Bauman Rare Books

A bibliophile's dream setting of floor-to-ceiling book shelves with a rarity at every turn. Titles can command five figures.

✉ 535 Madison Avenue ☎ 212/751-0011; www.baumanrarebooks.com
🚇 Fifth Avenue–53rd Street

Bruce Frank Beads and Ethnographic Art

Beads in more colors and shapes than you previously thought possible in materials ranging from bone to glass.

✉ 215 W 83rd Street ☎ 212/595-3746; www.brucefrankbeads.com
🚇 86th Street

Greenflea Indoor/Outdoor Markets

Part farmers' market, part flea market, it's held every Sunday, from 10am, hundreds of stands are laden with fresh produce, homemade goodies, clothing, posters, leather goods, vintage clothing and crafts. Also on Saturday in Greenwich Village (Greenwich Avenue and West 10th Street) 11–7.

✉ Columbus Avenue at 77th Street ☎ 212/239-3025; www.greenfleamarkets.com 🚇 79th Street

Sherry-Lehmann

A treasure trove of wines from around the world, from rare vintages to selections of ice wines, port, Madeira and sake, artfully displayed in their new flagship store.

✉ 505 Park Avenue at East 59th Street ☎ 212/838-7500; www.sherry-lehmann.com 🚇 Fifth Avenue–59th Street

ENTERTAINMENT

COMEDY
Stand-Up NY

Comics like Jerry Seinfeld, Dave Chappell and John Stewart honed their acts at this 175-seat club and sometimes still drop by.

✉ 236 West 78th Street ☎ 212/595-0850; www.standupny.com 🚇 79th Street

LECTURES AND PERFORMANCES
92nd Street Y

Readings and lectures by authors, industry and media leaders and other luminaries, along with concerts and other performances.

✉ 1395 Lexington Avenue ☎ 212/415-5500; www.92ndsty.org 🚇 96th Street

Symphony Space

Jazz and literary events, including short story readings by noted actors. A restored repertory house theater features indie and foreign films.

✉ 2537 Broadway ☎ 212/864-5400; www.symphonyspace.org 🚇 96th Street

Empire State Building to Greenwich Village

The Empire State Building and Greenwich Village epitomize the diverse attitudes of Manhattanites.

The Empire State Building stands between the Garment District and the Murray Hill neighborhood, once home to New York's best families. To the south are the Flatiron District, around the landmark building of that name (➤ 130) and New York's "Silicon Alley," Gramercy Park, a fashionable residential neighborhood on the east; and Chelsea, a village of tree-lined streets and art galleries on the west.

Originally "Greenwich Village" referred to the area bounded by the Hudson River and Fifth Avenue, 14th and Houston Streets. Today, "The Village" is generally understood to extend from the Hudson all the way to the East River. The East Village, still gritty compared with the West Village, centers on Tompkins Square Park

in "Alphabet City"—Avenues A, B, C and D. New York University is headquartered in buildings around Washington Square Park, but the institution has spread into the East Village and north to Union Square.

CHELSEA

The heart of Chelsea is around the intersection of 23rd Street and Eighth Avenue, busy with stores, restaurants, and art galleries since a 1990s regeneration made it one of Manhattan's most energetic neighborhoods. On Chelsea's western edge, in the former meat-packing district, many erstwhile warehouses were converted into galleries for the work of new artists, making the area a major showplace for emerging art. By the river, four early-1900s cruise-ship docks have been redeveloped as Chelsea Piers, offering sports activities, dining and shopping, beside the Hudson River.

➕ G16 ✉ Sixth Avenue to the Hudson River, 14th Street to the upper 20s 🚇 Canal Street

CHELSEA HOTEL

The Chelsea Hotel has played a major role in New York cultural life, providing accommodations for artistic and literary notables from Mark Twain to William Burroughs since opening in 1905. Featured in Andy Warhol's movie *Chelsea Girls* in the 1960s, the hotel also earned a place in punk rock history as the place where Sid Vicious murdered his girlfriend. The lobby has artworks from former guests.

www.chelseahotel.com

➕ G15 ✉ 222 W 23rd Street ☎ 212/243-3700 🕐 Lobby always open ✋ Free 🚇 23rd Street

EAST VILLAGE

After wealthy families like the Astors and the Vanderbilts moved north, immigrants from eastern Europe flooded into the East Village and the Lower East Side. Anarchist Emma Goldman published *Mother Earth* magazine on East 13th Street. Leon Trotsky ran a basement printing press on St. Mark's Place. The East Village was home to the beats in the 50s, hippies in the 60s, artists and and punk rockers in the 1970s. Gentrification arrived in the 1990s, though black leather, nose rings and tattoos are still far from unusual street attire.

Within the East Village are a host of ethnicities. One is the long-established ethnic pocket of Little Ukraine, and the section along East Sixth Street called Little Bombay for its plethora of inexpensive Indian restaurants.

✚ K17 ✉ Fifth Avenue to the East River, 14th and Houston streets 🚇 Astor Place

EMPIRE STATE BUILDING

Best places to see, ➤ 40–41.

FLATIRON BUILDING

The obvious way to maximize the potential of a triangular plot of land at Broadway and Fifth Avenue was to raise a triangular building on it, and with the Flatiron Building architect Daniel Burnham did exactly that. Completed in 1902, the structure, 286ft (87m) high, became the world's tallest building and was among the first in New York to use a steel-frame construction. This was a crucial element in the evolution of the skyscraper pioneered by Burnham 20 years earlier in Chicago. Beaux arts decoration on its limestone facade aids the building's lasting popularity.

🚩 H15 ✉ 175 Fifth Avenue ⊘ View from outside only ⊕ 23rd Street

FORBES GALLERIES

Larger-than-life publisher Malcolm Forbes—his adventures included ballooning across the U.S. and riding his powerful motorcycle at full speed along Fifth Avenue—invested some of a fortune estimated to be worth $700 million on the eclectic collection of priceless objects and worthless curios that fill these galleries, within the building that houses *Forbes* magazine.

Forbes died in 1990 and the fabulous gem-encrusted Fabergé eggs that once formed the centerpiece of the collection have been sold. Still on display, however, are more than 10,000 model soldiers in battle-ready poses, and more than 500 model boats and submarines and other objects.

www.forbesgalleries.com

🕂 H17 ✉ 62 Fifth Avenue ☎ 212/206-5548 🕓 Tue, Wed, Fri, Sat 10–4 ✋ Free 🚇 14th Street–Union Square

GRACE CHURCH

The gray stone suggests the European Middle Ages. Completed in 1846, the Episcopal church was designed by James Renwick, Jr. with a restrained Gothic Revival look, the earliest example of the style in New York. The success of Grace Church helped Renwick win the job of designing the more prestigious St. Patrick's Cathedral (➤ 94) and the first of the Smithsonian Institution buildings in Washington D.C. Peek inside to see the plaque installed in memory of the *Titanic* victims and the restored stained-glass windows.

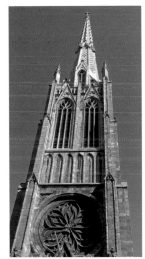

www.gracechurchnyc.org

🕂 J17 ✉ 802 Broadway ☎ 212/254-2000 🕓 Mon–Fri 10–4, Sun services ✋ Free 🚇 14th Street–NYU

GRAMERCY PARK

Enclosed by 19th-century brownstone townhouses intended to replicate some of the elegant squares of London, Gramercy Park is New York's only private park and entry is restricted to residents and guests of the Gramercy Park Hotel (52 Gramercy Park North).

A stroll of the park's perimeter passes several notable buildings: The National Arts Club (15 Gramercy Park South) was the home of state governor Samuel Tilden during his campaign against the notoriously corrupt Tweed ring in the 1870s before it became a club founded to support American artists. The Players Club (16 Gramercy Park South), marked by two ornamental theatrical masks designed by architect Stanford White, was a private club founded by actor Edwin Booth in what was his home. He is remembered by a statue in the park which depicts him immersed in the role of Shakespeare's *Hamlet*.

✚ J16 ✉ Between Irving Place and Lexington Avenue, bordered by E 21st and 22nd streets 🕓 Only open to local residents and guests of Gramercy Park Hotel ✋ Free 🚇 23rd Street

GREENWICH VILLAGE

Best places to see, ➤ 44–45.

LITTLE CHURCH AROUND THE CORNER

Formally known as the Church of the Transfiguration, this Episcopalian place of worship acquired its widely used epithet in 1870, when the pastor at a grander nearby church declined to conduct the funeral service of an actor and suggested that it be held instead at the "little church around the corner." New York thespians have looked kindly upon the daintily proportioned church ever since and several are remembered with their likeness in the stained-glass windows. The church sits behind a tranquil garden.

www.littlechurch.org

✚ H14 ✉ 1 E 29th Street ☎ 212/684-6770 🕓 Daily 9–5 ✋ Free 🚇 28th Street

MORGAN LIBRARY

Wanting to match Europe's great libraries, financier J. Pierpont Morgan built a collection of manuscripts, rare books and drawings and housed them in a library, designed by Charles McKim, erected next to his residence between 1902 and 1906. Among the many treasures gathered here are Gutenburg Bibles, a Shakespeare first folio, the sole signed manuscript of Milton's *Paradise Lost*, and handwritten works by Brahms, Mozart and Schubert.

No less imposing, however, is the setting. Morgan's study was once described as the "most beautiful room in America," but pales in comparison with the East Room, decorated by a mural-lined ceiling and a 16th-century Flemish tapestry above the fireplace.

www.morganlibrary.org
🚩 E12 ✉ 225 Madison Avenue ☎ 212/685-0008 ⏰ Tue–Thu 10:30–5, Fri 10:30–9, Sat 10–6, Sun 11–6 ✋ Expensive 🚇 33rd Street

ST. MARK'S-IN-THE-BOWERY

The Bowery was 17th-century Dutch governor Peter Stuyvesant's farm, and the Episcopalian Church of St. Mark's-in-the-Bowery was completed in 1799 on the site of what was probably Stuyvesant's chapel. Poets from Carl Sundburg to Allen Ginsberg have read here. It provides a useful local rendezvous for music and arts performances, as well as continuing its religious function. The now cobbled-over graveyard holds the bones of members of several generations of the Stuyvesant family.

🚩 K17 ✉ Second Avenue at E 10th Street ☎ 212/674-6377 ⏰ Call for times ✋ Free 🚇 Astor Place ❓ Poetry, dance and alternative arts events

THEODORE ROOSEVELT BIRTHPLACE

Theodore Roosevelt, the only U.S. president to have been a native of New York City, was born to a prominent family at this address in 1858, now a national historic site. Although the building of that time was demolished, what stands now is a detailed reconstruction of the childhood home of the nation's 26th president and contains many of the family's furnishings. A detailed chronology of Roosevelt's life outlines his numerous achievements, not least of which his rise to popularity after leading the so-called Rough Riders during the 1898 Spanish-American War.

www.nps.gov/thrb

✚ J16 ✉ 28 E 20th Street ☎ 212/260-1616 🕐 Tue–Sat 9–5; guided tours only 👆 Inexpensive 🚇 23rd Street

UKRAINIAN MUSEUM

Though small, the museum in the area of East Village known as Little Ukraine stores several thousand items of Ukrainian art, craft and culture. Traditional regional dress, folk art such as the hand-painted eggs known as *pysansky*, and contemporary painting and sculpture, along with changing exhibits, highlight various aspects of Ukrainian life past and present.

www.ukrainianmuseum.org

✚ J18 ✉ 222 East Sixth Street ☎ 212/228-0110
🕐 Wed–Sun 11:30–5 👆 Moderate 🚇 Astor Place

UNION SQUARE PARK

Renovated in the 1980s, Union Square Park holds a popular farmers' market four times a week where fruit, vegetables, cheese and bread are sold from stands.

Created in the early 1800s, Union Square was originally at the heart of fashionable New York life but, as high society moved northwards, it became a focal point for political protest. By 1927, police had taken to mounting machine-gun posts on surrounding rooftops and, in 1930, no fewer than around 35,000 people protested here against unemployment. After the terrorist attack of September 11, 2001, it became a gathering place for memorial services.

Ringing the park are fashionable eateries and food markets, New York University dormitories and the final home of Tammany Hall (100–102 East 17th Street).

✚ J16 ✉ Park Avenue and Broadway, 14th Street and 17th streets ✋ Free
🚇 14th Street–Union Square

HOTELS

▼▼▼ Affinia Manhattan ($$)

The public rooms of this 526-room hotel (formerly the Southgate Tower) are done in sumptuous velvets and gold. Newly renovated rooms are casual and spacious.

✉ 371 Seventh Avenue ☎ 212/563-1800; www.affinia.com Ⓜ 34th Street

Comfort Inn Manhattan ($$)

This branch of the nationwide chain predictably has higher rates than its far-flung counterparts but still represents good value for New York City, with tidy, comfortable rooms.

✉ 42 West 35th Street ☎ 212/947-0200 Ⓜ 35th Street

Hotel Stanford ($–$$)

The recently renovated bedrooms in this small hotel are small but good value. The bilingual staff caters to nearby Korean businesses.

✉ 43 West 32nd Street ☎ 212/563-1500; www.hotelstanford.com
Ⓜ 34th Street

▼▼▼ Inn at Irving Place ($$$)

A romantic small inn in two former 1830s townhouses near Gramercy Park.

✉ 56 Irving Place ☎ 212/533-4600; www.innatirving.com Ⓜ 14th Street

▼▼▼ Roger Williams ($$)

Light wood, bright colors and a design by Rafael Vinoly give this hotel a chic, West Coast feel. Many rooms have a view of the Empire State Building.

✉ 131 Madison Avenue ☎ 212/448-7000; www.rogerwilliamshotel.com
Ⓜ 33rd Street

Washington Square Hotel ($–$$)

Just off the square, this century-old hotel features recently renovated guest rooms with art deco-style furnishings. The lobby and intimate bar evoke Paris in the 1930s.

✉ 103 Waverly Place ☎ 212/777-9515; www.washingtonsquarehotel.com
Ⓜ West 4th Street–Washington Square

RESTAURANTS

Acme Bar and Grill ($–$$)
A variety of meat and fish dishes are given a spicy Cajun treatment and then smothered in hot and spicy, delicious fiery sauces.

✉ 9 Great Jones Street ☎ 212/420-1934; www.acmebarandgrill.com
🕐 Lunch and dinner Ⓢ Bleeker Street

August ($$)
Rustic and slightly cramped bistro with a courtyard that serves dishes from a wood oven. Mediterranean influenced with a contemporary twist.

✉ 359 Bleecker Street ☎ 212/929-4774; www.augustny.com 🕐 Brunch, lunch and dinner Ⓢ Christopher Street

💎💎 Blue Smoke ($$)
Danny Meyer brings "authentic pit barbecue" to New York with this restaurant. The rib sampler is a popular choice, which you can enjoy with a glass of wine or a beer. The lower floor is also a jazz venue.

✉ 116 East 27th Street ☎ 212/447-7733; www.bluesmoke.com 🕐 Lunch and dinner Ⓢ 28th Street

Bottino ($$–$$$)
See page 60.

Café Loup ($–$$)
This is an atmospheric, cozy French bistro with candlelit tables and delightful service.

✉ 105 W 13th Street ☎ 212/255-4746 🕐 Brunch, lunch and dinner Ⓢ 14th Street

Caffè Reggio ($)
Dark and atmospheric, this delightful coffee house has been popular since 1927.

✉ 119 MacDougal Street ☎ 212/475-9557; www.cafereggio.com
🕐 Daily Ⓢ West 4th Street

Chennai Garden ($)

South Indian kosher vegetarian fare with an extensive lunchtime buffet at an absurdly low price. The main menu is also good value. If you can't decide what to choose, opt for the combination plates.

✉ 129 E 27th Street ☎ 212/689-1999 🕐 Lunch and dinner
🚇 28th Street

Chumley's ($$)

See page 76.

♦ Corner Bistro ($)

Unpretentious locals' hangout where burger devotees will find heaven.

✉ 331 W 4th Street ☎ 212/242-9502 🕐 Lunch and dinner 🚇 14th Street–Eighth Avenue

Cowgirl Hall of Fame ($$)

Plaid-shirted staff ferry Tex-Mex fare and margaritas to diners seated beneath photos of legendary cowgirls.

✉ 519 Hudson Street ☎ 212/633-1133 🕐 Lunch and dinner
🚇 Christopher Street

Cucina Stagionale ($)

Simple, inexpensive, and very pleasing Italian food; be prepared to wait in line but the seasonal specialties are well worth the wait.

✉ 289 Bleecker Street ☎ 212/924-2707 🕐 Lunch and dinner
🚇 Christopher Street

Elephant and Castle ($–$$)

Wide-ranging and affordable food, from substantial omelettes to imaginative sandwiches and pasta dishes.

✉ 68 Greenwich Avenue ☎ 212/243-1400 🕐 Breakfast, lunch and dinner
🚇 14th Street

♦♦♦ Gotham Bar and Grill ($$$)

See page 60.

Gramercy Café ($)

The long expanses of glass make this café perfect for people-watching. This pleasant, bustling neighborhood place is a cross between a Paris bistro and a New York diner. Good food from a large menu; open 24 hours.

✉ 184 Third Avenue at 17th Street ☎ 212/982-2121 🕔 Breakfast, lunch and dinner 🚇 Union Square

Great Jones Café ($$)

Red beans and rice, burgers, sandwiches, plus Cajun classics served to the accompaniment of a pulsating jukebox.

✉ 54 Great Jones Street ☎ 212/674-9304; www.greatjonescafe.com

Home ($–$$)

On a sunny day, the garden makes a welcome setting for sampling the innovative takes on traditional American fare, such as spicy pork chops, chicken and dumpling stew, and grilled trout.

✉ 20 Cornelia Street ☎ 212/243-9579; www.recipesfromhome.com 🕔 Brunch, lunch and dinner 🚇 West 4th Street–Washington Square

Japonica ($$)

Spartan setting for substantial helpings of Japanese fare.

✉ 100 University Place ☎ 212/243-7752 🕔 Lunch and dinner 🚇 14th Street–Union Square

❦ Katz's Deli ($$)

New York's oldest deli is famous as the site of the hilarious "faking it" scene in *When Harry Met Sally*. Opened in 1888, it still sells good deli fare – great pastrami, corned beef, pickles, and hot dogs.

✉ 205 East Houston Street ☎ 212/254-2246; www.katzdeli.com 🕔 All day 🚇 Lower East Side–Second Avenue

Mitali East ($$)

Among the best of the Indian restaurants in the Little Bombay strip of East Sixth Street.

✉ 334 E Sixth Street ☎ 212/533-2508 🕔 Lunch and dinner 🚇 Astor Place

▼▼▼▼ One If By Land, Two If By Sea ($$$)

The converted 19th-century carriage house and wonderful piano music makes this a fine setting for a romantic candlelit dinner. Prix fixe menus only.

✉ 17 Barrow Street ☎ 212/255-8649; www.oneifbyland.com ⏰ Dinner 🚇 Christopher Street

▼▼▼ Otto Enoteca Pizzeria ($$)

Pizza is the specialty at this Italian restaurant. Chef Mario Batali serves some wonderful and unusual toppings, including fennel and swiss chard. Finish your meal in style with delicious gelato.

✉ 1 Fifth Avenue ☎ 212/995-9559; www.ottopizzeria.com ⏰ Lunch and dinner 🚇 West 4th Street

▼▼ Pastis ($$–$$$)

A re-creation of a Paris bistro. The food is French too, including *croque monsieur*, onion soup gratinée and *skate au beurre noir*.

✉ 9 Ninth Avenue ☎ 212/929-4844; www.pastisny.com ⏰ Breakfast, lunch and dinner 🚇 14th Street–Eighth Avenue

▼▼ Pearl Oyster Bar ($$–$$$)

Popular spot for seafood lovers, with an extensive menu that includes fried oysters and the chef's specialty of lobster roll.

✉ 18 Cornelia Street ☎ 212/691-8211; www.pearloyster.com ⏰ Lunch and dinner; closed Sun 🚇 West 4th Street

Pink Teacup ($)

The Southern American breakfasts featuring grits, bacon, and sausages are popular and good value; also soulfood dishes such as black-eyed peas and collard greens and barbecue.

✉ 42 Grove Street ☎ 212/807-6755; www.thepinkteacup.com ⏰ Breakfast, lunch and dinner 🚇 Christopher Street

▼▼▼ The Red Cat ($–$$)

Jimmy Bradley's red-painted, laid-back restaurant is ideal for dinner after a gallery visit in West Chelsea, with dishes from southern Italy such as sweet pea risotto cake.

✉ 227 10th Avenue ☎ 212/242-1122; www.theredcat.com 🕐 Dinner nightly from 5:30 🚇 23rd Street

The Spotted Pig ($–$$)

New York's first gastro-pub with food a cut-above staple bar fare. The menu includes mouthwatering Italian-based dishes of meat and seafood, with a few vegetarian options.

✉ 314 W 11th Street ☎ 212/620-0393; www.thespottedpig.com 🕐 Brunch, lunch and dinner 🚇 Christopher Street, 14th Street

Trailer Park Lounge & Grill ($)

Apart from the food, the real attraction here is the truckload of American kitsch: From the red-and-white check tablecloths to the photos of unfashionable celebrities.

✉ 271 W 23rd Street ☎ 212/463-8000; www.trailerparklounge.com 🕐 Lunch and dinner 🚇 23rd Street

SHOPPING

DEPARTMENT STORES AND SHOPPING CENTERS

Jeffrey New York
See page 80.

Macy's
See page 81.

Manhattan Mall
See page 81.

ART AND ANTIQUES

The End of History
Furniture, accessories and an extensive assortment of glassware from America, Italy, and Scandinavia arranged by color.
✉ 548½ Hudson Street ☎ 212/647-7598 🚇 Christopher Street

The Showplace
More than 135 art, antique dealers, and craft outlets.
✉ 40 W 25th Street ☎ 212/633-6063;www.nyshowplace.com 🚇 23rd Street

CLOTHES AND ACCESSORIES

Chelsea Girl Vintage Clothing

Stocks most things wearable from the 1920s to the 1970s, from silk dresses and lingerie to cashmere sweaters and businesswear, plus attention-grabbing accessories.

✉ 63 Thompson Street ☎ 212/643-1658 🚇 Houston Street

Daffy's

Bargains galore on designer clothes and kids' wear for those prepared to hunt. Many locations including this one near Union Square.

✉ 3 East 18th Street ☎ 212/529-4477; www.daffys.com 🚇 Union Square

Enz's

Fine handbags, jewelry and funky fashions with a touch of glam at this sweet little boutique in the East Village.

✉ 125 Second Avenue, between 7th and 8th streets ☎ 212/228-1943
🚇 Astor Place

The Family Jewels

Vintage men's suits and women's garb from 1920s evening gowns to 1970s "poly designer" dresses can be found among the racks of vintage clothing, along with hats, bags, shoes, and jewelry.

✉ 130 W 23rd Street ☎ 212/633-6020; www.familyjewelsnyc.com
🚇 23rd Street

Fisch For The Hip

Popular place to hunt down a choice piece of previously worn men's or women's designer wear, as well as to pore over a large stock of shoes and accessories.

✉ 153 W 18th Street ☎ 212/633-9053; www.fischforthehip.com
🚇 14th Street

Mandee

Cute, trendy styles that appeal to teens and twenty-somethings; handbags and accessories for everyone, all at discount prices.

✉ 48–50 W 14th Street ☎ 212/220-0095 🚇 Union Square

BOOKS, CDS AND RECORDS

Barnes and Noble

This is one of several Manhattan branches of this colossally well-stocked general bookstore that also boasts regular author readings and an inviting café with a fine selection of refreshments.

✉ 4 Astor Place ☎ 212/420-1322; www.bn.com 🚇 Astor Place

Biography Bookshop

As the name suggests, this store is packed from floor to ceiling with nothing but biographies.

✉ 400 Bleecker Street ☎ 212/807-8655 🚇 14th Street

Cosmic Comics

The proof that New York has inspired innumerable comic strips is here, amid thousands of new and used comic books, plus a wide range of comic-related paraphernalia.

✉ 10 E 23rd Street ☎ 212/460-5322; www.cosmiccomics.com 🚇 23rd Street–Broadway

Jazz Record Center

CDs, vinyl, videos, books, magazines, and much more pertaining to jazz, much of it hard to find elsewhere.

✉ 236 W 26th Street ☎ 212/675-4480; www.jazzrecordcenter.com 🚇 28th Street

Partners and Crime

Crime and mystery specialists stocking new, classic and out-of-print titles, some at bargain prices, and also hosting readings and signings from prominent crime authors.

✉ 44 Greenwich Avenue ☎ 212/243-0440; www.crimepays.com 🚇 Christopher Street

GIFTS, ODDITIES AND COLLECTIBLES

Exit 9

Emporium with a vast collection of wacky and oddball items.

✉ 64 Avenue A ☎ 212/228-0145; www.shopexit9.com 🚇 Astor Place or 2nd Avenue

ENTERTAINMENT

COMEDY
Comedy Cellar
This underground comedy club below the Olive Tree Café is evocative of 1960s Greenwich Village.
✉ 117 MacDougal Street ☎ 212/-254 3480; www.comedycellar.com
🚇 West 4th Street

LIVE MUSIC
Blue Note
Major jazz stars frequent this atmospheric club which can be very pricy to get in to.
✉ 131 W 3rd Street ☎ 212/475-8592; www.bluenote.net 🚇 W 4th Street

CBGB
Legendary launchpad for 1970s New York punk bands.
✉ 315 Bowery ☎ 212/982-4052; www.cbgb.com 🚇 Bleecker Street

The Fillmore at Irving Plaza
Premier medium-sized location for catching the new and well-known names of indie rock and club scene.
✉ 17 Irving Plaza ☎ 212/777-6800; www.irvingplaza.com
🚇 14th Street–Union Square

Village Vanguard
Long-serving atmospheric jazz venue with a deserved reputation for hearing the choice talents.
✉ 178 Seventh Avenue ☎ 212/255-4037; www.villagevanguard.com
🚇 14th Street

THEATER
Astor Place Theater
The outrageous Blue Man Group continues to perform their long-running show *Tubes* here.
✉ 434 Lafayette Street ☎ 212/254-4370; www.blueman.com
🚇 Astor Place

Lower Manhattan

Lower Manhattan is the oldest part of New York, with Dutch settlers arriving in the early 1600s. From the 1890s to the 1920s milllions of new immigrants were processed through Ellis Island and started their new lives in America.

There are many things to see and do in this area but an absolute must is to take a ferry ride out to the Statue of Liberty and Ellis Island. Wall Street, home of the New York Stock Exchange, is at the tip and nearby are the Civic Center and South Street Seaport Historic District, home to historic ships. The iconic Brooklyn Bridge was an example of pioneer engineering when it was built. Chinatown and SoHo lie north of the bridge and farther up is the Lower East Side.

No part of Manhattan resonates with the immigrant experience more than that neighborhood. From the mid-19th century through the peak years of immigration into the U.S., its high-rise tenements became crowded with successive waves of arrivals: Irish, Germans, East Europeans, and Jewish settlers who made the Lower East Side the largest Jewish settlement in the world by the 1920s. Today, Orchard Street is noted for its discount clothing outlets and nearby Essex Street for its fruit and vegetable market. The World Trade Center site remains unbuilt on, a huge hole in this part of the island. After the buildings were leveled in 2001, tightened security made touring in this part of Manhattan more difficult, and landmark sights and buildings such as the New York Stock Exchange and the Woolworth Building are no longer accessible to the public.

LOWER
EAST SIDE
SOHO
CHINATOWN
LOWER
MANHATTAN
FINANCIAL
DISTRICT

AMERICAN NUMISMATIC SOCIETY

Money through the ages and throughout the world is the main subject of the exhibitions here. Displays include an assortment of maps, coins, and paper currency spanning 3,000 years from ancient Greece to modern times. Adjoining galleries showcase medals and other decorations. Exhibitions are currently held nearby at the Federal Reserve Bank of New York, 33 Liberty Street.

➕ J22 ✉ 96 Fulton Street ☎ 212/571-4470 🕐 Mon–Fri 10–4
🚇 Fulton Street

BATTERY PARK

Providing 22 acres (9ha) of welcome greenery on the edge of the Financial District, Battery Park also holds more than its fair share of New York history, some of the details of which are supplied by the texts affixed to its lampposts. Created in the 18th century, the park's name stems from the cannons that once lined State Street, now framing the park but previously marking the Manhattan shoreline. Castle Clinton National Monument, site of the ticket booth for Statue of Liberty ferries, was completed in 1811. The Sphere, a sculpture damaged in the attack on the World Trade Center, is on display at the east side of the park.

➕ H24 ✉ Battery Place and State Street to New York Harbor 🕐 Always open; visit during daylight 👆 Free 🍴 Snack stands ($) 🚇 Bowling Green

BROOKLYN BRIDGE

Completed in May 1883, the Brooklyn Bridge provided the first fixed link between Brooklyn and Manhattan and, with a total length of 6,016ft (1,834m), it became the world's longest suspension bridge. The twin Gothic stone arches that rise 272ft (83m) give the bridge great aesthetic appeal, though the most memorable aspect is the view of the Manhattan skyline as you cross from the Brooklyn side. Walkers, roller-bladers, and joggers regularly cross the bridge; in 1884, 21 elephants made the crossing in a stunt led by circus owner P. T. Barnum.

⊞ K22 ✉ Between Manhattan and Brooklyn 🕐 Always open ✋ Free
🚇 Brooklyn Bridge–City Hall

CHINATOWN

Around 150,000 people, mostly Chinese but also Vietnamese, Cambodians and Laotians, live in Chinatown's tight-knit streets, lined by restaurants, herbalists stores and stands laden with exotic foodstuffs. Chinatown became established during the 1890s but began expanding beyond its traditional boundaries when the easing of immigration restrictions in the 1960s brought a major influx of settlers from Hong Kong and Taiwan. It's now the largest Chinatown in the U.S., with Canal its main street.

⊞ K20 ✉ Broadway to Allen, Delaney to Worth 🚇 Canal Street

CITY HALL

When designed in 1803, City Hall was intended to mark the northern edge of Manhattan, but nine years later at the time of its completion, it was already engulfed by fast-expanding New York. Built in a mixture of Federal and French Renaissance styles, the dainty building retains its civic role, the oldest building in the nation that still functions as a city hall. Inside, the mayor and council members go about their business and temporary exhibitions document various aspects of city history.

➕ J21 ✉ Broadway at Murray Street
☎ 212/788-3000 🕐 Tours by advance reservation
✋ Free 🚇 Brooklyn Bridge–City Hall

ELLIS ISLAND IMMIGRATION MUSEUM

Twelve million people from 120 ethnic groups became U.S. citizens after passing through Ellis Island, the country's major point of entry during the peak period of immigration from Europe that lasted from the 1890s to the 1920s. Examined for contagious diseases, signs of madness, and quizzed on their work skills, most arrivals found Ellis Island a bewildering and frightening experience, particularly after a long and uncomfortable sea voyage, and some were forced to spend time living in the cramped dormitories before being admitted to the U.S. (approximately 2 percent were denied entry altogether).

An excellent gathering of exhibits and oral histories documents the emotions of the immigrants and goes some way to suggesting the chaos that prevailed in the arrivals hall, where 5,000 people a day once entered carrying their possessions and speaking little English but looking forward to a new life.
www.ellisisland.com

➕ J24 (off map) ✉ Ellis Island ☎ 212/269-5755 (ferry and ticket information); 212/363-3200 (general information) 🕐 Daily 9:30–5, longer in summer ✋ Museum free; ferry expensive 🍴 Café ($) 🚢 Ferry from Battery Park, via Liberty Island

FEDERAL HALL NATIONAL MEMORIAL

Federal Hall, in the heart of the Financial District, was completed in 1842 and is a good example of Greek Revival architecture. Beneath an impressive rotunda, the airy interior holds assorted historical displays. One exhibit remembers the Inauguration of George Washington as the nation's first president in 1789, in the previous Federal Hall which stood on this site.

➕ J23 ✉ 26 Wall Street ☎ 212/826-6888 🕐 Mon–Fri 9–5 ✋ Free 🚇 Wall Street

FINANCIAL DISTRICT

Wall Street is at the heart of New York's Financial District. Many of the high-rise towers of commerce that dot the neighborhood sit side-by-side with markers to a time when populated New York barely reached beyond today's Greenwich Village. Peek inside the 18th-century St. Paul's Chapel (on Broadway facing Fulton Street) to see George Washington's pew, and pay respects to Alexander Hamilton, the U.S.'s first treasurer, buried in the graveyard of Trinity Church (on Trinity Place, facing Wall Street).

Within the neoclassical facade that overpowers Broad Street is the high-tech money market of the New York Stock Exchange, where brokers, reporters and pagers stride purposefully around the 37,000sq ft (3,440sq m) of trading floor. Since September 11, 2001, visitors are no longer allowed inside.

✚ J23 ✉ South of Chambers and Fulton streets 🚇 Bowling Green, Broad Street, Cortland Street, Fulton Street, Nassau Street, Rector Street, South Ferry, Wall Street or Whitehall Street

FRAUNCES TAVERN MUSEUM

A stately house built in 1719 and turned into a tavern in 1762, Fraunces Tavern was a hotbed of revolutionary activity until the Revolutionary War. At the end of the war, George Washington made a famously emotional farewell to his officers in an upstairs room, which is now the historical centerpiece of the present-day restored tavern.

www.frauncestavernmuseum.org

✚ J23 ✉ 54 Pearl Street ☎ 212/425-1778 🕐 Mon–Sat 12–5
🎫 Inexpensive 🍴 Restaurant ($$–$$$) 🚇 Bowling Green, South Ferry, Wall Street or Whitehall Street

LITTLE ITALY

Today, only a few thousand Italians remain in Little Italy, an area that between 1890 and 1924 absorbed more than 100,000 immigrants from Sicily and southern Italy. Mulberry Street became awash with Italian restaurants and cafés.

Over subsequent decades, Italians from the area became ingrained in the social fabric of New York life. Italian–American New Yorkers who grew up in Little Italy still regard it as a spiritual home. Now, the neighborhood is being squeezed from two sides—Chinatown expanding from the east and gentrification from the fashionable NoLita (North of Little Italy).

Undoubtedly the best time to visit Little Italy is during the Feast of St. Gennaro in September, when the compact area regains something of its effervescent past.

✚ J19 ✉ Bounded by Canal–Houston streets and Elizabeth–Lafayette streets Ⓒ Canal Street

LOWER EAST SIDE TENEMENT MUSEUM

A cramped, rat-infested apartment shared with several other families was what awaited many arrivals to the Lower East Side in the 19th century—and for most it was far better than the conditions they had left behind in a troubled, oppressive Europe.

To get an inkling of early immigrant life in New York, visit this excellent museum which occupies an 1863 tenement building and is furnished to replicate the living conditions of the time. Companion exhibitions reveal diverse facets of local life and document the otherwise seldom acknowledged hardships faced by the Lower East Side's arrivals from Asia and Latin America.

www.tenement.org

➕ K19 ✉ 108 Orchard Street ☎ 212/431-0233 🌐 Guided tours only: Tue–Fri 1–4, Sat–Sun 11–4:30; tours vary, reservations advised ✋ Expensive 🚇 Delancey Street ❓ Guided walks Apr–Dec Sat and Sun

MUSEUM OF CHINESE IN THE AMERICAS

A small but absorbing documentation of the settlement of Chinese in the U.S. The main exhibits are a mix of family photos, items from Chinese-run businesses, and objects of symbolic significance; temporary exhibitions examine aspects of the Chinese diaspora.

www.moca-nyc.org

➕ J20 ✉ 70 Mulberry Street ☎ 212/619-4785 🌐 Tue–Sun 12–6 (Fri until 7) ✋ Inexpensive 🚇 Canal Street

MUSEUM OF JEWISH HERITAGE

At the south end of Battery Park, this museum of the Holocaust occupies a granite building topped by a distinctive six-tiered roof. Displays trace Jewish life and history from persecution in Europe to the creation of Israel and the growth of Jewish communities.

www.mjhnyc.org

➕ H23 ✉ 36 Battery Place ☎ 646/437-4200 🌐 Sun–Tue, Thu 10–5:45, Wed 10–8, Fri 10–5 ✋ Moderate 🚇 Bowling Green ❓ Lectures, films

NATIONAL MUSEUM OF THE AMERICAN INDIAN

This collection of the Smithsonian Institution has largely moved to new quarters in Washington, D.C., leaving the George Gustav Heye Center to display special exhibits in New York. The museum occupies an elegant 1907 beaux arts building designed by Cass Gilbert that formerly served as the U.S. Custom House, worth a visit in its own right. Inside are renowned murals of New York Harbor by Reginald Marsh.

www.nmai.si.edu

✚ J23 ✉ 1 Bowling Green ☎ 212/514-3700 🕐 Mon–Wed, Fri–Sun 10–5, Thu 10–8 ✋ Free 🚇 Bowling Green

NEW MUSEUM OF CONTEMPORARY ART

Like the avant-garde art within, the bold, white modern building challenges its surroundings in the Lower East Side. There are several major exhibits a year featuring international artists.

✚ K19 ✉ 235 Bowery at Prince Street ☎ 212/219-1222 🕐 Wed–Sun 12–6 (Thu–Fri until 10pm) ✋ Expensive 🚇 Bowery

NEW YORK CITY FIRE MUSEUM

The intriguing story of the city's fires and those who tried to put them out is told here over three floors with an entertaining collection of horse-drawn carriages, hosepipe nozzles, axes, ladders, dramatic photos, and New York's first fire bell.

www.nyctiremuseum.org

✚ I110 ✉ 270 Spring Street ☎ 212/691-1303 🕐 Tue–Sat 10–5, Sun 10–4 ✋ Donation: moderate 🚇 Spring Street

NEW YORK CITY POLICE MUSEUM

The fabled mean streets of New York have produced more than their share of notorious villains, and many of them are recorded here, as are the officers who brought them to justice. Displays include vintage motorcycles, historic badges and documents, and an exhibit chronicling the role of the NYPD on September 11, 2001.

www.nycpolicemuseum.org

➕ J23 ✉ 100 Old Slip ☎ 212/480-3100 🕐 Mon–Sat 10–5 ✋ Moderate donation suggested 🚇 Whitehall Street

OLD ST. PATRICK'S CATHEDRAL

Old St. Patrick's Cathedral, completed in 1815, served the spiritual needs of the Irish population that inhabited the immediate area before the ethnic turnaround that transformed the neighborhood into Little Italy. The Gothic-style cathedral lost its place as the city's Roman Catholic see with the consecration of its far grander namesake in Midtown Manhattan (➤ 94) in 1879. Though unspectacular, the intimate interior makes for a few welcome minutes of respite from the city frenzy.

www.oldsaintpatricks.com

➕ J19 ✉ 263 Mulberry Street ☎ 212/226-8075 🕐 Call for times ✋ Free 🚇 Prince Street

SHRINE OF ELIZABETH ANN SETON

Elizabeth Ann Seton, who founded the Sisters of Charity, the first order of nuns in the U.S. in 1812, was canonized in 1975 for her philanthropic works, becoming the first American-born Roman Catholic saint. This simple but well-preserved Georgian and Federal-style house was her home from 1801 to 1803, prior to her conversion to Catholicism in 1805. It now serves as a church, where Mass is held daily.

www.setonshrine.com

➕ J24 ✉ 7 State Street ☎ 212/269-6865 🕐 Call for times ✋ Free 🚇 Whitehall Street

SOHO

In one of the transformations that regularly regenerate Manhattan neighborhoods, the previously derelict 19th-century factory buildings of SoHo, with cheap-to-rent loft studios, became the center of a vibrant art community in the 1960s and then of the world art market a few years later. Some galleries remain, alongside chic clothing and shoe stores and restaurants, but loft space is too expensive for up-and-coming artists. Most SoHo residents today are lawyers and other professionals.

➕ J19 ✉ South of Houston Street, between Sixth Avenue and Broadway
🚇 Prince Street or Spring Street

SOUTH STREET SEAPORT HISTORIC DISTRICT

Through the 18th and 19th centuries, the center of Manhattan's thriving maritime trade was around the cobblestone area known as the South Street Seaport Historic District on the East River. A mixture of mall stores and restaurants now sit alongside historic ships and nautically themed museums. The area and its numerous old ships—among them the 1911 *Peking*, a four-masted cargo vessel which can be boarded and toured—can fill a few enjoyable hours. The museum traces the history of the port of New York. Events takes place in and around the area during the year.
www.southstseaport.org

➕ K22 ✉ Water and South streets; museum at 12 Fulton Street
☎ 212/748-8600 (museum) 🕐 Varies ✋ Moderate 🍴 Numerous restaurants and cafés ($–$$) 🚇 Fulton Street or Broadway–Nassau

STATUE OF LIBERTY

Best places to see, ➤ 52–53.

TRIBECA

Echoing the gentrification that transformed neighboring SoHo in the 1970s, TriBeCa was, during the early 1980s, steadily colonized by artists who created living and studio space in Federal-style

residences and industrial buildings that once housed the city's food wholesalers. Soon, the area boasted a good elementary school and developers created chic loft apartments. TriBeCa's streets acquired fashionable restaurants and expensive boutiques, though it still has a community feel. It's now home to an annual spring film festival started by Robert De Niro.

✚ H20 ✉ South of Canal Street, between Broadway and the Hudson River
Ⓜ Chambers Street or Franklin Street

WOOLWORTH BUILDING

The world's tallest building for 16 years, the Woolworth Building—once headquarters of the retail organization—was opened in 1913 by president Woodrow Wilson who flicked a switch and bathed the building in the glow of 80,000 electric bulbs. Leering gargoyles decorate the tower, 792ft (241m) high. The lobby (closed to the public) has an elaborate interior and sculptured caricatures of the building's architect, and its original owner, F.W. Woolworth.

✚ J21 ✉ 233 Broadway 🚇 City Hall or Park Place

WORLD TRADE CENTER SITE

Almost twice the height of the highest buildings around them, the twin towers of the World Trade Center became a symbol of New York and of a U.S.-driven global economy. On September 11,

2001, the destruction of the towers by hijacked passenger planes immediately claimed almost 3,000 lives. Following the attack, the site became a place of pilgrimage and neighboring St. Paul's Chapel was bedecked with handwritten tributes to, and mementos of, the dead. New commercial buildings nearby reflect the Financial District's determination to recover from the tragedy. Plans for redevelopment of the 16-acre (6.5ha) site and a permanent memorial are still in flux.

www.nycvisit.com

✚ H22 ✉ Church, Barclay, Liberty and West streets; viewing area at Liberty Street ☎ 212/484-1222 🚇 Cortlandt Street

HOTELS

Cosmopolitan Hotel TriBeCa ($)

Quiet, modern rooms and a great location for exploring Lower Manhattan make this small hotel excellent value.

✉ 95 West Broadway at Chambers Street ☎ 212/566-1900; www.cosmohotel.com 🚇 Chambers Street

▼▼▼ Embassy Suites Hotel New York ($$)

Part of the extensive Battery Park city entertainment and retail complex, there are 363 two-room suites in this waterfront hotel that has an impressive atrium and views of the Hudson River.

✉ 102 North End Avenue ☎ 212/945-0100 🚇 Cortlandt Street

▼▼▼ Holiday Inn Downtown ($–$$)

A rare hotel in Chinatown that makes the most of its limited space with well-appointed if modest rooms.

✉ 138 Lafayette Street ☎ 212/966-8898 🚇 Canal Street

Hotel on Rivington ($$–$$$)

This 21-story tower with its sleek rooms and chic restaurant is in the vanguard of the hip scene on the Lower East Side. Floor-to-ceiling windows in every room give fabulous views over Manhattan.

✉ 107 Rivington Street ☎ 212/475-2600; www.hotelonrivington.com
🚇 Essex Street–Delancey Street

▼▼▼ SoHo Grand ($$$)

A stylish, sophisticated hotel designed to reflect the eclectic neighborhood around it, from the Coke-bottle staircase and cast-iron detailing to the chic guest rooms in natural materials.

✉ 310 West Broadway ☎ 212/965-3000; www.sohogrand.com
🚇 Canal Street

Wall Street Inn ($$)

This small hotel with early American decor offers deals on weekends, when business travelers to nearby Wall Street leave.

✉ 9 South William Street ☎ 212/747-1500; www.thewallstreetinn.com
🚇 Wall Street

RESTAURANTS

Bennie's Thai Cafe ($)

Very affordable, very delicious Thai fare in a relaxed setting and always packed.

✉ 88 Fulton Street ☎ 212/587-8930 ⏰ Lunch and dinner
🚇 Fulton Street

Chanterelle ($$$)

Make a reservation well in advance for one of New York's longest-established fashionable eateries, where even the extensive cheese choice is the stuff of gourmets' dreams.

✉ 2 Harrison Street ☎ 212/966-6960 ⏰ Lunch and dinner; closed Sun and Mon lunch 🚇 Franklin Street

Franklin Station ($$)

Popular locals' haunt with a mixture of French and Southeast Asian cooking.

✉ 222 West Broadway ☎ 212/274-8525; www.franklinstationcafe.com
⏰ Lunch and dinner 🚇 Franklin Street

Fuleen ($$)

This Chinese seafood specialty restaurant prepares Hong Kong-style fare and is noted for its creamy Dungeness crab.

✉ 11 Division Street ☎ 212/941-6888 ⏰ Lunch and dinner
🚇 Canal Street

Golden Unicorn ($–$$)

A favorite for large family banquets or big parties. Great selection of dishes from savory appetizers through dim sum to duck, fresh fish and bean curd.

✉ 18 East Broadway ☎ 212/941-0911 ⏰ Breakfast, lunch and dinner
🚇 East Broadway

Great NY Noodle Town ($)

Noodles in many forms and with a choice of meat, seafood and vegetables to accompany them.

✉ 28 Bowery ☎ 212/349-0923 ⏰ Lunch and dinner 🚇 Grand Street

HSF ($$)

One of the better Chinatown stops for lunchtime dim sum.

✉ 46 Bowery ☎ 212/374-1319 🕓 Breakfast, lunch and dinner
🚇 East Broadway

Joe's Shanghai ($)

Shanghai dishes but best known for its steamed buns, a selection
of which make an inexpensive snack or a fuller meal.

✉ 9 Pell Street ☎ 212/233-8888 🕓 Lunch and dinner 🚇 East Broadway

Mandarin Court ($)

A lively spot for dim sum; be prepared to shout your order.

✉ 61 Mott Street ☎ 212/608-3838 🕓 Breakfast, lunch and dinner
🚇 Canal Street

Mexican Radio ($)

Great value Mexican food served in a tiny cantina that makes a
great hideaway when exploring Little Italy and SoHo.

✉ 19 Cleveland Place ☎ 212/343-0140 🕓 Lunch and dinner
🚇 Spring Street

♦♦♦ Montrachet ($$$)

Classic French dishes prepared with modern flair, and a huge
selection of wines.

✉ 239 West Broadway ☎ 212/219-2777 🕓 Lunch and dinner
🚇 Franklin Street

♦♦ Nam ($$$)

See page 61.

♦♦♦♦ Nobu ($$$)

See page 61.

Omen ($$$)

Enjoy the relaxed atmosphere here as you sample carefully
prepared Japanese dishes.

✉ 113 Thompson Street ☎ 212/925-8923 🕓 Dinner 🚇 Spring Street

Pho Bang ($–$$)

Vietnamese food with plentiful variations of *Pho*, or beef noodles. Adventurous diners will find much to thrill their tastebuds.

✉ 3 Pike Street ☎ 212/233-3947 🕐 Lunch and dinner
🚇 Grand Street

Salaam Bombay ($$)

A cut above most Indian eateries with a stylish ambience and extensive menu; the lunch buffet is expensive but good value.

✉ 319 Greenwich Street ☎ 212/226-9400; www.salaambombay.com
🕐 Lunch and dinner 🚇 Chambers Street

Sweet-n-Tart ($)

Popular restaurant noted for its dim sum but also serves a range of Chinese dishes and delicious desserts.

✉ 20 Mott Street ☎ 212/964-0380 🕐 Breakfast, lunch and dinner
🚇 East Broadway

▼▼▼ Zoe ($$)

A bright, attractive SoHo loft setting and an inspired, eclectic menu help make this one of the city's favorite SoHo restaurants.

✉ 90 Prince Street ☎ 212/966-6722 🕐 Lunch, dinner and brunch
🚇 Prince Street

SHOPPING

CLOTHES AND ACCESSORIES

Alife Rivington Club

Make a fashion statement with the latest trainers (athletic shoes) at this trendy specialty footwear boutique. Limited edition styles from America, Europe and Japan in hot colors and designs.

✉ 158 Rivington Street, between Clinton and Suffolk streets ☎ 212/375-8128 🚇 Essex Street–Delancey Street

Canal Jean Co

Brave the pulsating music and garish lighting for cut-rate jeans, sportswear, T-shirts, accessories, and more.

✉ 718 Broadway ☎ 212/226-3663 🚇 Eighth Street

Century 21
The aisles are crammed with discounted designer fashions at this multilevel department store opposite the World Trade Center site.
✉ 22 Cortlandt Street ☎ 212/227-9092; www.c21stores.com 🚇 Fulton Street

INA
Barely used designer garments, shoes, and accessories.
✉ 101 Thompson Street ☎ 212/941-4757 🚇 Prince Street

Morgane le Fay
Dramatic women's clothes and ball gowns.
✉ 67 Wooster Street ☎ 212/ 219-7672 🚇 Spring Street

ENTERTAINMENT

CINEMA
Angelika Film Center
American independent and international art films are the specialty at this six-screen complex.
✉ 18 West Houston Street ☎ 212/995-2000; www.angelikafilmcenter.com
🚇 Bleeker Street

LIVE MUSIC
Knitting Factory
The cutting-edge sounds of jazz, ska, funk, and rock's avant-garde percolate through this musician-friendly venue.
✉ 74 Leonard Street ☎ 212/219-3132; www.knittingfactory.com
🚇 Franklin Street

Mercury Lounge
Popular showcase for the best local and rising national indie bands.
✉ 217 E Houston Street 🖭 212/260 4700 🚇 Second Avenue

THEATER
Performing Garage
Venue for an experimental theater group whose founding members include Willem Dafoe.
✉ 33 Wooster Street ☎ 212/966-9796 🚇 Canal Street

Excursions

The Bronx, Brooklyn, Queens and Staten Island, sometimes dismissively called the "Outer Boroughs," have become more than suburban accommodation for those who live and work in Manhattan.

As Manhattan real estate prices push out the young, the newly arrived and the artistic, new areas such as Astoria in Queens and DUMBO (Down Under Manhattan Bridge Overpass) in Brooklyn are growing vibrant. In addition, each of the boroughs has its own sense of identity, history and cultural worth and each, in its own way, has something special to offer the curious traveler. Certainly a visit to one or a number of them will provide a fuller picture of the real New York City.

The Bronx

Spanning rundown areas such as the South Bronx, and comfortable residential areas such as Riverdale, the Bronx tends to be neglected by visitors and New Yorkers alike. Nonetheless, with the Bronx Zoo and Yankee Stadium, the borough holds two of the city's major attractions as well as several minor ones. Two important gardens are in the Bronx: the New York Botanical Gardens (Bronx River Parkway and Fordham Road), with the largest conservatory in the U.S., and Wave Hill Gardens (West 249th Street and Independence Avenue), with stately beeches and views of the Hudson. Historical sites include the one-time home of author Edgar Allen Poe (East Kingsbridge Road) and the elegant 18th-century Van Cortlandt Mansion (Broadway at West 246th Street), built for a family prominent in politics and farming, now a showplace of English, Dutch and Colonial period furnishings.

BRONX ZOO

The largest city zoo in the U.S., the Bronx Zoo holds spacious replicated habitats inhabited by antelopes, rhinos, elephants, snow leopards, monkeys, gorillas, and many more creatures from around the world. Among the special attractions is the 6.5-acre (2.6ha) Gorilla Forest, with two troops of lowland gorillas.

www.bronxzoo.com

✉ Bronx River Parkway, Fordham Road

☎ 718/367-1010 🕐 Apr–Oct daily 10–5; Nov–Mar daily 10–4:30 💰 Expensive

🚇 Pelham Parkway

YANKEE STADIUM

Home of the New York Yankees baseball team since its 1923 completion, Yankee Stadium has seen tens of thousands of spectators thrilling to "the winningest team in baseball." Babe Ruth and Joe di Maggio played here, and Pope Paul VI conducted Mass at the stadium in 1965. It's often filled to its capacity of 57,000. Monument Park, beyond the outfield fence, is filled with memorials to Yankee greats. The team will move to its new, state-of-the-art stadium in 2009.

www.yankees.com

✉ Junction of 161st Street and River Avenue ☎ 718/293-6000

🏏 Baseball season Apr–Oct 🖐 Variously priced match tickets

🚇 161st Street–Yankee Stadium

Brooklyn

Physically, only the East River divides Brooklyn from Manhattan but this borough retains a distinct identity, in part a legacy of its origins as a self-governing city

separate from Manhattan. In a mood of regional unity that followed the opening of the Brooklyn Bridge, the people of Brooklyn voted by a narrow margin to give up their autonomy in 1898.

BRIGHTON BEACH

The decline of residential Brighton Beach more or less matched that of nearby Coney Island until the 1980s, when a Russian emigre community started building here. Now nicknamed Little Odessa, the area is filled with Cyrillic signs advertising caviar and vodka and scores of lively Russian restaurants.

🚇 Brighton Beach

BROOKLYN MUSEUM OF ART

Among New York museums, the Brooklyn Museum of Art is second in size only to Manhattan's Metropolitan Museum of Art. Its exuberant beaux arts building was created by the revered New York firm of McKim, Mead and White between 1897 and the 1920s and only partially completed.

The Brooklyn Museum can easily consume several hours, if not a full day. The Egyptian collections are outstanding and include more than 500 items of stunningly decorated sarcophagi,

sculpture, and wall reliefs. Mosaics, ceramics, and bronzes feature among the substantial horde of artifacts from ancient Greece and Rome, and 12 monumental reliefs from 9th-century BC Abyssinia form the core of the Middle East displays.

From more recent periods, a fine collection of paintings and period rooms highlight changing American tastes from Colonial times onward. Among the canvases are one of Gilbert Stuart's iconographic portraits of George Washington, painted in the 1790s. Impressive works from the Hudson River School artists culminate in Albert Bierdstadt's enormous evocation of nature in *Storm in the Rockies*. Its collection of American watercolors includes important works by John Singer Sargent, Winslow Homer and many 20th-century practitioners. The museum also mounts changing exhibits showcasing new and emerging artists.

www.brooklynmuseum.org

✉ 200 Eastern Parkway at Prospect Park ☎ 718/638-5000 🕐 Wed–Fri 10–5, Sat and Sun 11–6; first Sat of month 11–11 💷 Moderate 🚇 Eastern Parkway

a walk

around Brooklyn Heights

Tidy streets lined with brownstone houses and fabulous Manhattan views help make Brooklyn Heights one of the classiest neighborhoods in the borough.

Exit from Borough Hall subway station onto Joralemon Street.

At 209 Joralemon Street, Brooklyn Borough Hall has been the area's administrative base since the early 1800s but its current Greek Revival form dates from 1848. On the other side of Joralemon Street, the Brooklyn Municipal Building was completed in 1926.

Turn right onto Court Street and left onto Montague Street.

Lined by shops and restaurants, Montague Street is the main commercial strip of Brooklyn Heights. On the corner with Clinton Street, the Church of St. Anne and the Holy Trinity is a finely proportioned rendition of a Gothic church in local brownstone topped by a soaring spire. Finished in 1847, the church holds the first stained-glass window to be designed in the U.S. (open weekdays 12–2).

Walk a block north to Pierrepont Street.

At 128 Pierrepont Street is the elegant home of the Brooklyn Historical Society (➤ 175).

Return to Montague Street and walk west.

Before the opening of the Brooklyn Bridge (➤ 148–149), the western end of Montague Street held the departure point for a ferry service to Manhattan's Financial District, an excellent view of which can be found along the Esplanade (also known as the Promenade) running north from Montague Street and lined with inviting benches.

Follow the Esplanade north and turn right onto Orange Street.

Immediately past the intersection with Hicks Street stands the Plymouth Church of the Pilgrims (➤ 177).

Distance 1 mile (1.5km)
Time 1–4 hours
Start point Joralemon Street ✚ M24
End point Orange Street ✚ L23
Lunch Five Front ($$) ✉ 5 Front Street ☎ 718/625-5559

BROOKLYN BOTANIC GARDEN

Occupying a one-time waste dump, the Brooklyn Botanic Garden fills 52 acres (21ha) with 12,000 plant species. Passing magnolias and cherry trees, the footpaths weave through lushly landscaped surroundings linking the various sections. Perennial favorites are the Rose Garden, Herb Garden, and the exquisite 1914 Japanese Garden complete with pond, stone lanterns, and viewing pavilion.

Inside the three-part Steinhart Conservatory are plants from the world's deserts, rainforests, and warm temperate regions, while fans of bonsai will find much to admire in the C. V. Starr Bonsai Museum.

www.bbg.org

🖂 1000 Washington Avenue
☎ 718/623-7200 🕓 Mar–Oct Tue–Fri 8–6, Sat–Sun 10–6; Nov–Feb Tue–Fri 8–4:30, Sat–Sun 10–4:30 🚻 Moderate (free Tue and Sat 10–12)
🚇 Eastern Parkway

BROOKLYN HISTORICAL SOCIETY

This elegant and spacious red-brick, Queen Anne-style building was specially designed in 1881 to house the collection of the Society, founded in 1863, when Brooklyn was the commercial and cultural center of Long Island.

Exhibits focus on Brooklyn cultural themes such as the changing ethnic makeup of the city, the rise and fall of the naval dockyards, the opening of the Brooklyn Bridge, the creation of Coney Island, or the 1955 World Series-winning Brooklyn Dodgers.

www.brooklynhistory.org

✉ 128 Pierrepont Street

☎ 718/222-4111 🕐 Wed–Sun noon–5 ✋ Moderate 🚇 Borough Hall or Court Street

CONEY ISLAND

Up until the 1940s, Coney Island not only promised New Yorkers a day by the sea for the price of a subway ride, but provided the additional allure of state-of-the-art fairground rides and assorted lowbrow theatrical events, from peepshows to freakshows. Up to a million people a day flocked here to be seduced by the roller-coasters and rifle ranges, or simply to stroll the coastal Boardwalk munching a hotdog from the celebrated Nathan's Famous.

After decades of neglect, Coney Island has been recognized as a living piece of Americana. Diverse exhibits from its glory days are displayed at the Coney Island Museum, which also organizes local walking tours. Nearby, the towering Cyclone roller-coaster continues to provide gravity-defying rides and forms part of the thrills and spills offered at the Astroland Amusement Park. More sedate ways to pass the time include the New York Aquarium, featuring performing dolphins and sea lions and a re-created Pacific coastal habitat complete with walruses, seals, penguins, and sea otters.

✉ Surf Avenue between W 37th Street and Ocean Parkway ☎ 718/372-5158 (museum) 🚇 Stillwell Avenue–Coney Island 🖐 Museum moderate, Aquarium expensive

NEW YORK TRANSIT MUSEUM

Housed in a former subway station, the New York Transit Museum shows off the finely crafted art deco air vents and ceramic station nameplates indicative of the care that went into creating what became the world's second-largest mass transit system. Arranged alongside a platform, walk-through restored subway cars from 1904 to 1964 demonstrate stylistic changes and technological innovations. A simulated intersection is the scene for an interactive display of buses.

www.mta.info/museum

✉ Boerum Place and Schermerhorn Street ☎ 718/694-1600 🕐 Tue–Fri 10–4, Sat–Sun noon–5 🖐 Moderate 🚇 Boerum Place–Schermerhorn Street

PLYMOUTH CHURCH OF THE PILGRIMS

From its founding in 1850, a stage in the "Underground Railroad" that helped runaway slaves escape to Canada, the Plymouth Church of the Pilgrims became the best-known public meeting place in Brooklyn. The church was noted above all for the sermons of Henry Ward Beecher, resident clergyman for some 40 years until his death in 1887 and a popular speaker who promoted the abolition of slavery and women's suffrage, while his writings controversially supported Darwin's theory of evolution. He's remembered by a statue in the adjoining garden. Some of the windows in the church were designed by Louis Comfort Tiffany. The church is now of the Congregational denomination.

www.plymouthchurch.org

✉ Hicks and Orange streets ☎ 718/624-4743 🕓 Guided tour only: Mon–Fri 10–4, Sun 11–2; advance reservations required ✋ Call for prices 🚇 Clark Street

PROSPECT PARK

Manhattan's Central Park may be better known, but many Brooklynites regard it simply as a trial run for Prospect Park, laid out by the same design team of Frederick Law Olsted and Calvert Vaux and completed in the late 1880s. The 526-acre (213ha) park encompasses lawns, meadows, streams and ponds, and provides the community with a bucolic space for jogging, strolling and picnicking, plus many special events throughout the year. In 1892, the park's main entrance at Grand Army Plaza gained a Memorial Arch, a triumphal marker to the fallen of the Civil War. The Prospect Park Zoo is on the Flatbush Avenue side. A free trolley operates on weekends.

✉ Prospect Park West, Flatbush, Parkside and Ocean avenues ☎ 718/965-8999 (events) 🕐 Visit during daylight hours ✋ Free 🚇 Grand Army Plaza

THE DEFENDERS OF THE UNION 1861 18

Queens

With 2 million people spread across 112sq miles (290sq km), Queens is in part all-American suburbia, but also holds an ethnic mix of long-established Italians and Greeks alongside more recently arrived Koreans, Indians, Chinese, and Japanese.

The single area best representing Queens past and present is Flushing, which holds a large Asian population yet retains the Friends Meeting House (137–16 Northern Boulevard) and the nearby Bowne House (32–01 Bowne Street) that both date from the 17th century. In 1939, New York demonstrated its recovery from the Depression with a World's Fair in Flushing Meadows-Corona Park (immediately east of Flushing), its success prompting a second fair in 1964. Among the surviving items are Philip Johnson's New York State Pavilion Building and the 140ft (43m) Unisphere, depicting the earth and its satellites. Nearby are the USTA National Tennis Center, home of the U.S. Open, and Shea Stadium, home of baseball's Mets.

Across the East River from the Upper East Side, Astoria is one of the world's largest Greek communities and claims countless Greek bakeries, cafés, and restaurants. In the days before the industry shifted to Hollywood, the nascent U.S. film industry was based in New York, and in 1919 the company that evolved into Paramount Pictures opened a studio in Astoria. The American Museum of the Moving Image now stands on the studio's site (intersection of 35th Avenue and 36th Street). The museum records the era with costumes, props, film-making equipment, and vintage movie posters, and features many more general exhibits on film and television themes.

Staten Island

Totally unlike any other part of New York City, Staten Island is dominated by hills, trees and greenery. Its slow pace and pastoral appearance could be reasons enough to visit, but it also holds interesting historical sites and an excellent collection of Tibetan religious art, and sees regular open-air events throughout the summer.

ALICE AUSTEN HOUSE

Given a camera by her uncle in 1876, Alice Austen went on to take around 8,000 photographs that provide a remarkable documentary of turn-of-the-20th-century American domestic life. Despite the quality of her photos, Austen remained unknown and only shortly before her death in 1952 did her photos find recognition, following the publication of some of them in *Life* magazine. A short film describes Austen's life, and some of her possessions and photos fill this attractive bayside home (a National Historic Landmark, originally built in 1690) into which the Austen family moved in 1868.

www.aliceausten.org

✉ 2 Hylan Boulevard ☎ 718/816-4506 ⏰ Thu–Sun 12–5. Closed Jan and Feb ✋ Inexpensive 🚌 S51

CONFERENCE HOUSE

The stone-built Conference House, originally known as the Billopp House and built for a retired British naval captain, dates from 1680. It earned its new name as the venue of the only attempt to broker a peace between the Americans and the English after the Declaration of Independence. Held in September 1776, the negotiations proved futile but provided a reason to turn the building, which served for a time as a rat-poison factory, into a museum with period furnishings and an intriguing display about the failed talks.

www.theconferencehouse.org

✉ 7455 Hylan Boulevard ☎ 718/984-0415 ⏰ Fri–Sun 1–4. Closed mid-Dec to Mar ✋ Inexpensive 🚌 S78

GARIBALDI MEUCCI MUSEUM

Later to become one of the founders of independent, unified Italy, Giuseppe Garibaldi lived on Staten Island for two years in the 1850s, having been forced to flee his homeland. Employed as a candle-maker, Garibaldi lived in this house that then belonged to Italian-American inventor Antonio Meucci. Letters, personal items, and other knick-knacks document Garibaldi's period of occupancy. A companion exhibit describes Meucci's life and achievements, not least his inventing of the telephone—an idea he unfortunately failed to patent.

✉ 420 Tompkins Avenue ☎ 718/442-1608 🕓 Tue–Sun 1–5 ✋ Moderate
🚌 S78

HISTORIC RICHMOND TOWN

The fruit of 50 years of gathering and restoring 28 17th- to 19th-century buildings on a 100-acre (40ha) site, Richmondtown Village provides a telling peek into bygone days. Period-attired local history enthusiasts lead visitors around the buildings, often furnished with their original occupants' possessions, describing the trials and tribulations of Staten Island life in times past. During summer, the craft workshops are staffed by blacksmiths, shoemakers and carpenters demonstrating the old skills.

The oldest of the many noteworthy buildings is the 1695 Voorlezer's House, a church, school, and home for the lay minister of the Dutch Reform Church. The far grander Greek Revival Third County Courthouse dates from 1837 and functions as a visitor center. Across Center Street, the Historical Museum provides an absorbing overview of the island's changing fortunes and the industries, from brewing to oyster harvesting, that have underpinned its often fragile economy.

www.historicrichmondtown.org

✉ 441 Clarke Avenue ☎ 718/351-1611
🕐 Jul–Aug Wed–Sat 10–5, Sun 1–5;
Sep–Jun Wed–Sun 1–5 💵 Moderate
🚌 S74

JACQUES MARCHAIS MUSEUM OF TIBETAN ART

A Wheel of Life, incense burners, ritual objects, and other items from the world's Buddhist cultures (all accompanied by informative explanatory text) are among the collection of curiosities gathered in this stone cottage designed to resemble part of a Tibetan mountain temple. The collection started when Edna Coblentz discovered 12 Tibetan figurines in the family attic, brought home by her seaman grandfather. In the 1930s and 1940s, as a Manhattan gallery owner she adopted the professional name of Jacques Marchais, and collected Tibetan art. She then used the name Jacqueline.

www.tibetanmuseum.org

✉ 338 Lighthouse Avenue ☎ 718/987-3500 ⓧ Wed–Sun 1–5 ✋ Moderate
🚌 S74

SNUG HARBOR CULTURAL CENTER

While its tree-lined lanes would be enjoyable to stroll in any circumstances, the 83 acres (33ha) of this restored sailor's community are also dotted with preserved 19th-century Greek Revival buildings. The Newhouse Center for Contemporary Art displays works by living American artists in changing exhibitions; and the Veteran's Memorial Hall is a venue of concerts and recitals. In summer, the South Meadow stages outdoor concerts while the attractive Sculpture Park is filled with

interesting works. The Botanic Garden and a small Children's Museum provide more reason to linger in an area originally known as Sailor's Snug Harbor, a hospital and rest home created to provide refuge for "decrepit and worn-out sailors."

www.snug-harbor.org

✉ 1000 Richmond Terrace ☎ 718/448-2500 ⓧ Dawn–dusk ✋ Grounds free; galleries inexpensive 🚌 S40

Index

Acknowledgments

The Automobile Association would like to thank the following photographers, companies and picture libraries for their assistance in the preparation of this book.

Abbreviations for the picture credits are as follows – (t) top; (b) bottom; (c) centre; (l) left; (r) right; (AA) AA World Travel Library.

6/7 View from the Empire State Building, AA/R Elliot; **8/9** Statue of Liberty, AA/R Elliot; **10/11** NY Sky line, AA/C Sawyer; **10l** Brooklyn Bridge, AA/C Sawyer; **10r** Central Park, AA/C Sawyer; **11b** Union Square, AA/C Sawyer; **12l** Bagels, AA/S McBride; **12r** Honey AA/C Sawyer; **13t** Katz's Deli, AA/S McBride; **13c** Hotdog, AA/C Sawyer; **13b** Grand Central Oyster Bar, AA/S McBride; **14/5** Chelsea seafood restaurant, AA/S McBride; **14l** Trattoria Greenwich Village, AA/S McBride; **14r** Chelsea District, AA/C Sawyer; **15b** Cocktails, Photodisc; **16/7** Empire State Building, AA/S McBride; **17t** Brooklyn Bridge, AA/C Sawyer; **17b** Times Square, AA/C Sawyer; **18t** Staten Island ferry, AA/C Sawyer; **18b** Jefferson Market Library, AA/S McBride; **19** Museum of Modern Art, MOMA/Timothy Hursley 2005; **20/1** Grand Central terminal, AA/S McBride; **25** Polish Day Parade, AA/C Sawyer; **28/9** Taxis, AA/D Corrance; **31** Telephone, AA/C Sawyer; **34/5** Central Park, AA/S McBride; **36t** Central Park, AA/ P Kenward; **36b** Central Park, AA/ P Kenward; **36/7** Central Park, AA/S McBride; **37t** Central Park, AA/S McBride; **38t** Chrysler building, AA/C Sawyer; **38/9** Chrysler building, AA/C Sawyer; **40t** Empire States Building, AA/S McBride; **40b** View from the Empire State Building, AA/C Sawyer; **41** Empire State Building, AA/D Corrance; **42t** Grand Central, AA/S McBride; **42b** Grand Central, AA/S McBride; **42/3** Grand Central, AA/S McBride; **44** Washington Square, AA/S McBride; **45t** Greenwich Village, AA/R Elliot; **45b** Washington Square, AA/C Sawyer; **46/7** Guggenheim Museum, AA/S McBride; **47t** Guggenheim Museum, AA/C Sawyer; **48t** Metropolitan Museum of Art, AA/D Corrance; **48/9** Metropolitan Museum of Art, AA/R Elliot; **49b** Metropolitan Museum of Art, AA/C Sawyer; **50** Museum of Modern Art, MOMA/Timothy Hursley 2006; **51** Museum of Modern Art, MOMA/Timothy Hursley 2005; **52** Statue of Liberty, AA/C Sawyer; **53** Statue of Liberty, AA/R Elliot; **54b** Times Square, AA/C Sawyer; **54/5** Times Square, AA/C Sawyer; **55t** Times Square, AA/C Sawyer; **56/7** American Museum of Natural History, AA/R Elliot; **58/9** Grand Central Oyster Bar, AA/S McBride; **61** Pizza Chef, AA/S McBride; **62t** Cooper-Hewitt National Design Museum, AA/C Sawyer; **62/3** American Museum of Natural History, AA/C Sawyer; **63t** Guggenheim Museum, AA/C Sawyer; **64/5** View from the Empire State building, AA/C Sawyer; **66/7** American Museum of Natural History, AA/C Sawyer; **68/9** Shopping bag, AA/C Sawyer; **70/1** Times Square, AA/C Sawyer; **73** Metropolitan Opera House/Lincoln Center for the Performing Arts, AA/P Kenward; **74/5** Clubbing, Brand X Pics; **76/7** Tribeca Odeon Restaurant, AA/C Sawyer; **78/9** Carlyle Hotel, AA; **79b** Waldorf Astoria Hotel, AA/C Sawyer; **80/1** Woman shopping, AA/M Jourdan; **81t** Macy's, AA/C Sawyer; **82/3** Gramercy Park, AA/C Sawyer; **85** Carnegie Hall, AA/P Kenward; **86/7** Carnegie Hall, AA/C Sawyer; **87t** Daily News Building AA/C Sawyer; **88/9** Museum of Art and Design, Museum of Art and Design/Alan Klein; **90** NY Public Library, NY Public Library/James Resnick; **91** NY Public Library, NY Public Library/Don Pollard; **92t** Rockefeller Center, AA/C Sawyer; **92b** Rockefeller Center, AA/C Sawyer; **93t** Roosevelt Island, AA/C Sawyer; **93b** Roosevelt Island cable car, AA/R Elliot; **94/5** St Patrick's Cathedral, AA/D Corrance; **95t** St Patrick's Cathedral, AA/C Sawyer; **95b** Seagram Building, AA/C Sawyer; **96/7** Trump Tower, AA/R Elliot; **97b** United Nations, AA/C Sawyer; **106/7** American Museum of Natural History, AA/E Rooney, **108** Cloisters, AA/C Sawyer; **109** Cathedral Church of John the Divine, AA/C Sawyer; **110t** Cooper Hewitt Museum, AA/C Sawyer; **110/11** Library at Columbia University, AA/R Elliot; **112/3** Dakota Building, AA/C Sawyer; **114** Frick Collection, AA/R Elliot; **115** Gracie Mansion, AA/C Sawyer; **116/7** East Harlem, AA/C Sawyer; **117b** Lincoln Center, AA/C Sawyer; **118t** Museum of the City of NY, AA/R Elliot; **118/9** Metropolitan Museum of Art, AA/C Sawyer; **120** Whitney Museum of American Art, AA/P Kenward; **127** Chelsea District, AA/C Sawyer; **128/9** Chelsea Hotel, AA/C Sawyer; **130** Flatiron Building, AA/D Corrance; **131l** Grace Church AA/N Lancaster; **131r** Grace church, AA/C Sawyer; **132** Gramercy Park, AA/C Sawyer; **134** Pierpont Morgan Library. AA/C Sawyer; **135** St Marks in the Bowery church, AA/C Sawyer; **136/7** Union Square, AA; **148** Battery Park, AA/C Sawyer; **149** Chinatown, AA/C Sawyer; **150/1** Federal Hall National Monument, AA/P Kenward; **152** Stock Exchange, AA/C Sawyer; **153t** Little Italy, AA/R Elliot; **153b** Little Italy, AA/C Sawyer; **155** New York City Fire Museum, AA/R Elliot; **156** St Patrick's Cathedral, AA/C Sawyer; **158/9** South Street Seaport, AA/S McBride; **160** Ground Zero, AA/C Sawyer; **166/7** Brooklyn Botanical Garden, AA/P Kenward; **169** Bronx Zoo, AA/R Elliot; **170** Brooklyn, AA/R Elliot; **171t** Brighton Beach, AA/R Elliot; **171b** Brooklyn Museum of Art, AA/C Sawyer; **172/3** Brooklyn Heights, AA/D Corrance; **174/5** Brooklyn Botanic Gardens, AA/C Sawyer; **176/7** Plymouth Church of the Pilgrims, AA/C Sawyer; **178/9** Prospect Park, AA/C Sawyer; **180/1** Staten Island/Conference House, AA/C Sawyer; **182/3** Staten Island/Richmondtown Historic Restoration, AA/C Sawyer; **183b** Staten Island/Snug Harbor Cultural Center, AA/C Sawyer.

Every effort has been made to trace the copyright holders, and we apologise in advance for any accidental errors. We would be happy to apply the corrections in the following edition of this publication.

Street Index

Sight Locator Index

This index relates to the maps on the covers. We have given map references to the main sights in the book. Some sights may not be plotted on the maps.

Dear Reader

Your comments, opinions and recommendations are very important to us. Please help us to improve our travel guides by taking a few minutes to complete this simple questionnaire.

You do not need a stamp (unless posted outside the UK). If you do not want to cut this page from your guide, then photocopy it or write your answers on a plain sheet of paper.

Send to: **The Editor, AA World Travel Guides, FREEPOST SCE 4598, Basingstoke RG21 4GY.**

Your recommendations...

We always encourage readers' recommendations for restaurants, nightlife or shopping – if your recommendation is used in the next edition of the guide, we will send you a **FREE AA Guide** of your choice from this series. Please state below the establishment name, location and your reasons for recommending it.

_____
_____
_____
_____
_____

Please send me **AA Guide** _____

About this guide...

Which title did you buy?

AA _____

Where did you buy it? _____

When? m m / y y

Why did you choose this guide? _____

_____
_____
_____

Did this guide meet your expectations?

Exceeded ☐   Met all ☐   Met most ☐   Fell below ☐

Were there any aspects of this guide that you particularly liked? _____

_____
_____
_____

continued on next page...

Is there anything we could have done better? _____
_____
_____
_____

About you...
Name (*Mr/Mrs/Ms*) _____
Address _____
_____
_____Postcode

Daytime tel nos _____
Email _____

Please only give us your mobile phone number or email if you wish to hear from us about
other products and services from the AA and partners by text or mms, or email.

Which age group are you in?
Under 25 ☐   25–34 ☐   35–44 ☐   45–54 ☐   55–64 ☐   65+ ☐

How many trips do you make a year?
Less than one ☐   One ☐   Two ☐   Three or more ☐

Are you an AA member? Yes ☐   No ☐

About your trip...
When did you book? m m / y y   When did you travel? m m / y y

How long did you stay? _____

Was it for business or leisure? _____

Did you buy any other travel guides for your trip?

If yes, which ones? _____
_____
_____

Thank you for taking the time to complete this questionnaire. Please send it to us as soon as
possible, and remember, you do not need a stamp (*unless posted outside the UK*).

> **AA** Travel Insurance call 0800 072 4168 or visit www.theAA.com